D1414183

WHEN
THE
SKY
fell

WHEN THE SKY fell

In Search of Atlantis

RAND and ROSE FLEM-ATH

Introduction by Colin Wilson

First published in 1995 by
Stoddart Publishing Co. Limited
34 Lesmill Road
Toronto, Canada
M3B 2T6
Tel. (416) 445-3333
Fax (416) 445-5967

Canadian Cataloguing in Publication Data

Flem-Ath, Rose
When the sky fell : in search of Atlantis

Includes index.
ISBN 0-7737-2863-5

1. Atlantis.   I. Flem-Ath, Rand.   II. Title.

GN751.F54 1995   001.9′4   C95-930053-8

Every reasonable effort has been taken to obtain reprint permissions. The publisher will gladly receive information that will help rectify any inadvertent errors or omissions in subsequent editions.

Cover design: Bill Douglas/The Bang
Typesetting: Tony Gordon Ltd.
Printed and bound in Canada

Stoddart Publishing gratefully acknowledges the support of the Canada Council, the Ontario Ministry of Culture, Tourism, and Recreation, Ontario Arts Council, and Ontario Publishing Centre in the development of writing and publishing in Canada.

For the last of the untamed places . . .

Contents

List of Illustrations and Maps

Illustrations

1. Earth's interior
   SOURCE: Frederic Golden, *The Moving Continents* (New York: Charles Scribner's Sons, 1972), 70.
   Reprinted with the permission of Atheneum Books for Young Readers, an imprint of Simon & Schuster Children's Publishing Division from THE MOVING CONTINENTS by Frederic Golden. Copyright © 1972 Frederic Golden.
2. Cross-section showing the asthenosphere
   SOURCE: Peter J. Wyllie, *The Way the Earth Works* (London: John Wiley, 1976), 19. Reprinted with permission.
3. An Anasazi "solar" cord
   SOURCE: Thomas Y. Canby, "The Anasazi: Riddles in the Ruins," *National Geographic* (November 1982), 580.
   Reprinted with permission: Christopher A. Klein, © National Geographic Society.

Maps

1a and 1b. Agricultural origins altitude:
   a) Vavilov's eight centres of agricultural origins;
   b) land over 1,500 metres above sea level
   SOURCE: Nikolai Ivanovich Vavilov, "The origin, variation, immunity and breeding of cultivated plants; Selected writings of N.I. Vavilov," trans. K. Starr Chester, *Chronica Botanica* 13, no. 1–6 (1951).

2. Tropical agricultural origins
   SOURCE: Author drawn.

3. Crescent of land where the world's first civilizations appeared
   SOURCE: Author drawn.

4. Land over 1,800 metres above sea level and four mountains referred to in North American native mythology
   SOURCE: Author drawn.

5. The Southern Hemisphere between 52,600 and 11,600 years ago
   SOURCE: Author drawn.

6a and 6b. The lines of greatest and least latitude changes after the last earth crust displacement
   SOURCE: Author drawn.

7. "The Navel of the Earth" in the Arctic Ocean
   SOURCE: William Fairfield Warren, *Paradise Found: The Cradle of the Human Race at the North Pole; A Study of the Prehistoric World* (Boston: Houghton, Mifflin & Co., 1885), 227.

8. A U.S. Navy projection showing Antarctica in the belly of the world's ocean
   SOURCE: U.S. Naval Support Force, *Introduction to Antarctica*, 4th rev. (Washington, D.C.: U.S. Government Printing Office, 1969), centrepiece.

9. Antarctica compared to the lower forty-eight states of the United States
   SOURCE: Author drawn.

10. Antarctic glaciation and annual snowfall
   Source for glaciation:
   A.N. Strahler, *Introduction to Physical Geography* (New York and London: John Wiley, 1973), 355.

SOURCE: Author modified, based upon U.S. Naval Support Force, *Introduction to Antarctica*.

23a and 23b. The city of Atlantis
Source: Author modified, based upon Plato, *Timaeus, Critias, Cletophon, Menezenus, Epistles*, trans. R.D. Bury (1929; reprint, Cambridge, MA: Harvard University Press; London: William Heinemann Ltd., 1975), insert.

24a and 24b. The city of Atlantis compared to London
SOURCE: Author drawn.

25a to 25d. Finding the city of Atlantis
SOURCE: Author modified, based upon *The Mitchell Beazley Atlas of the Oceans*.

26a and 26b. The 1559 Hadji Ahmed map of North America compared to a modern map
SOURCE: Author modified, based upon Charles H. Hapgood, *Maps of the Ancient Sea Kings: Evidence of Advanced Civilization in the Ice Age* (Philadelphia: Chilton Book Company, 1966), 100.

27. The Hadji Ahmed map of North America
SOURCE: Author drawn.

28. The Piri Re'is map of 1513
SOURCE: Author modified, based upon Charles H. Hapgood, *Maps of the Ancient Sea Kings*, 37–38, 254–59.

29. Kircher's Egyptian map of Atlantis
Source: Athanasius Kircher, *Mundus Subterraneus* (Amsterdam, 1678), 82.

30. Kircher's Atlantis versus an ice-free Antarctica
Source: Author modified, based upon Kircher, *Mundus Subterraneus*; and *The Mitchell Beazley Atlas of the Oceans*.

31. The world according to Pomponius Mela
Source: E.H. Bunbury, *A History of Ancient Geography* (Century Co., 1932; reprint, New York: Dover Pub. Inc., 1959), 369.

Acknowledgements

We have been fortunate in this journey of discovery to have been joined on the trail and encouraged by other adventurers. The late Charles Hapgood honoured us with his keen support in the very early years. This book is a development of his discoveries in geology and ancient cartography, and we are indebted for the time he took in correspondence with us. On August 3, 1977, he wrote: "I am astonished and delighted by your article which arrived here today. Believe it or not, it is the *first* truly scientific exploration of my work that has ever been done. You have found evidence for crust displacement that I did not find." We wish he could be here to see the end result. To our friend, Martin Schnell, we offer many thanks for many hours of fascinating conversation over the kitchen table. Also Brian Stocker and Josie Killeen, who spent a lot of time at that same table. Paul William Roberts first had the courage to open the door for us and Nelson Doucet invited us in. John Anthony West and Graham Hancock held out an encouraging hand from the beginning. Colin Wilson offered fresh enthusiasm and was generous with his time in writing our introduction. Don Bastian, David Kilgour, and Lynne Missen have been professional beyond the dreams of any new author and we are grateful for their skilful guidance in making this book the best it could be.

Introduction

by Colin Wilson

The thesis of this book is so simple and yet so startling that it will almost certainly earn Rand and Rose Flem-Ath a permanent place in the history of the earth sciences.

It can be summarized in seven words: Antarctica is the lost continent of Atlantis.

Expressed this simply, it is bound to arouse a groan: we've heard it all before. Since congressman Ignatius Donnelly published *Atlantis: The Antediluvian World* in 1882, there have been more than a thousand books on the subject. Yet I cannot emphasize too strongly that the Flem-Aths are working with new and highly convincing evidence, and that there is every indication that they have got it right. Within the decade or so, their theory could, quite simply, be accepted as scientific fact. I am certainly willing to stick out my neck and admit that I am more than 90 percent convinced. And since the Flem-Aths have only hinted at some of this evidence — some of which, indeed, is extremely recent — let me attempt a brief summary.

The Flem-Aths describe how, in 1953, Albert Einstein became enthusiastic about the work of Charles H. Hapgood, professor of the history of science at Keene State College in New Hampshire, and how Hapgood launched his theory five years later in a book called *Earth's Shifting Crust*. Hapgood's concern was to explain the great mystery of the Ice Ages and, incidentally, some of the great catastrophes — floods, earthquakes, and so on — that geology tells us have punctuated the history of our earth.

Hapgood started from the hypothesis that the great polar ice caps unbalance the earth, like putting a heavy rug, rolled up in a ball, into a spin dryer. But the bulge at the equator helps to counteract this effect through centrifugal force — it is all a little like balancing the wheel of a car by attaching a small weight to its rim. But when Hapgood's friend James Campbell calculated the forces involved, he found that the stabilizing effect of the equatorial bulge was thousands of times greater than the destabilizing effect of the polar ice caps. But, Campbell suggested, the ice caps might well have the force to pull the earth's crust askew, if that crust is a floating layer, like the skin that forms on cold soup. There is scientific evidence to show that Hudson Bay was once at the North Pole, while a study of magnetism in the rocks of England showed that the British Isles were once more than two thousand miles south of their present position. India and Africa were once covered with a sheet of ice, yet Siberia escaped. Was it not possible, asked Hapgood, that an "ice age" did not, in fact, affect the whole earth, but only parts of it — those parts that moved into polar regions?

It was while he was working on Earth's Shifting Crust that Hapgood heard of another intriguing mystery: an ancient map, dated 1513, that depicted Antarctica — three centuries before it was "discovered." Maps like this, known as portolans (meaning from port to port), were used by sailors in the Middle Ages. But the 1513 map showed Antarctica as it had been before the ice. And soundings through the ice (1958–1978) showed that the ancient maps were accurate. Hapgood and his students carried out a lengthy survey of portolans, and in his Maps of the Ancient Sea Kings (1966), Hapgood announced his conclusion that there had been a sophisticated maritime civilization at the time when the first walled cities were being built in the Middle East.

It was unfortunate for Hapgood that mediaeval portolans — particularly the one known as the Piri Re'is Map — had been used by writers like Erich von Daniken and Louis Pauwels in books whose purpose was to suggest that "ancient astronauts" from distant planets had landed on earth thousands of years ago; von Daniken even suggested that they had been responsible for building the Great Pyramid and erecting the statues of Easter Island. There was an understandable tendency to tar Hapgood with the same brush used on von Daniken.

Another writer, Immanuel Velikovsky (less cranky than von Daniken but less scientific than Hapgood), had also gained a worldwide following with his theory that some of the great natural catastrophes on our planet had been caused by a huge comet, ejected from Jupiter, which came close to the earth and caused volcanic eruptions and tidal waves before it settled down as Venus. Rather less widely known was the theory of a maverick Egyptologist named Schwaller de Lubicz that ancient Egyptian civilization had been founded by survivors from Atlantis. He argued that this civilization had reached a high level of sophistication in far too short a time — between 3200 B.C. and 2500 B.C. — to have started from scratch. The reaction of scientists to such theories was to dismiss them wholesale as lunacy.

In the United States, John Anthony West, a writer on Egyptology, became fascinated by Schwaller de Lubicz's theories. After all, if we ignore that ancient astronaut theory and concentrate on known facts, then we appear to be left with some quite solid evidence: (1) that Antarctica was both mapped and inhabited more than six thousand years ago; and (2) that a sophisticated maritime civilization, which was acquainted with China and Russia as well as South America, was in existence at the same time.

Schwaller de Lubicz had adduced a great deal of evidence from Egyptian pyramids and temples to show that ancient Egyptian astronomy was based upon a knowledge that seemed to date back to a civilization thousands of years older than Egypt. West was particularly interested in de Lubicz's suggestion that the Sphinx could have been built by the survivors of this civilization — we may as well call it Atlantis — thousands of years earlier than previously thought, and that the weathering of the Sphinx is due not to wind-blown sand but to water that poured down long before Egypt was a desert. This, West felt, should be easy enough to prove or disprove. After expounding the theory in a book called *Serpent in the Sky* (1979), West finally succeeded in persuading Robert Schoch, a geologist from the University of Boston, to accompany him to Egypt to look at the evidence. Schoch's own research convinced him that the Sphinx had been eroded by water, and at a geological conference in San Diego in 1991 he created a sensation by announcing his conclusion that the Sphinx could be as old as 7000 B.C. and that it was not, therefore, as most Egyptologists believe, contemporary with the Great Pyramid (about 2500 B.C.). West made a television program about these results that caused controversy when it was broadcast in the United States in the autumn of 1993.

But there was more interesting evidence on the way. A construction engineer named Robert Bauval had become intrigued by the problem of the arrangement of the three pyramids at Giza. To the eye of an engineer, the third — built by Menkaura — was oddly out of alignment. A solution came to him when he was looking at the stars one night in the desert. The three stars in the belt of the constellation of Orion (sacred to the ancient Egyptians) were in precisely the same pattern as the pyramids.

In his book The Orion Mystery (1994), Bauval presents his own theory that the so-called "ventilation shafts" of the Great Pyramid were aimed like gun barrels at Orion, so the soul of the dead pharaoh could fly there like a projectile. Bauval's evidence is far too complex to summarize here, but one of his casual remarks is of great interest in this context. The earth's "wobble" (known as "precession") causes the stars to appear to change position over the centuries, then return to their original position.

Bauval argued that the evidence indicates that the Great Pyramid could be regarded as a kind of "star clock" whose hands first pointed to the date 10,450 B.C. — the time when the three stars of Orion would have been seen in precisely the position of the three pyramids. Bauval actually mentions Plato and Atlantis, pointing out that the clairvoyant Edgar Cayce mentioned 10,500 B.C. as the date of the destruction of Atlantis, and suggesting that the Great Pyramid may have been at least planned at this date. It seems odd that Bauval should be prepared to stick his neck out — in a basically scientific study — to mention Atlantis (and, worse still, Edgar Cayce) unless he is also inclined to believe that there is some connection between ancient Egypt and what he calls "the Atlantis event."

At the end of Maps of the Ancient Sea Kings, Hapgood suggests that one fruitful line of research into his ancient maritime civilization might be the study of comparative mythology and the "virtual identity of the great systems of mythology throughout the world." I do not know whether this hint was the origin of the Flem-Aths' decision to pursue the mythological approach. If so, it has certainly been richly justified, for the sections on mythologies are among the most impressive parts of this book. What the Flem-Aths have done is to place squarely on the map of scientific speculation the notion that Antarctica could have been Atlantis, and that the secrets of the legendary lost civilization may lie beneath its ice. If they prove correct — or even partly correct — they will have changed our whole view of human history.

WHEN
THE
SKY
fell

Chapter One Adapt, Migrate, or Die

On May 8, 1953, an elderly professor with a fondness for the violin sat down at his desk in Princeton, New Jersey, and wrote a letter to Charles H. Hapgood, an obscure instructor at a small New England college. The professor was Albert Einstein and the topic of the letter was a theory of Hapgood's that had "electrified" the great physicist. Einstein wrote:

> I find your arguments very impressive and have the impression that your hypothesis is correct. One can hardly doubt that significant shifts of the crust of the earth have taken place repeatedly and within a short time.[1]

Thus began one of the least-known correspondences in the history of science.

Charles Hutchins Hapgood, a graduate of Harvard College and the Harvard Graduate School of Arts and Sciences, was born in New York City on May 17, 1904. After graduating, Hapgood travelled to Germany where his studies at the University of Freiburg coincided with Adolf Hitler's rise to power. When the Second World War erupted, he returned to the United States and joined the Office of Strategic Studies (OSS, the forerunner of the CIA) as a civilian with inside knowledge of Nazi Germany. After the war, Hapgood became a professor of anthropology and the history of science at Keene State College in New Hampshire.

In the early 1950s he began formulating his theory of earth crust displacement, a project that would occupy him for nearly twenty years. His first contact with Einstein was followed by several letters.

1

The great physicist believed that Hapgood was on the right track. At a meeting in January 1955, only months before his death, Einstein told Hapgood that the "gradualistic notions common in geology were . . . merely a habit of mind, and were not necessarily justified by the empirical data."[2]

In his foreword to Hapgood's book, *Earth's Shifting Crust*, Einstein wrote:

> A great many empirical data indicate that at each point of the earth's surface that has been carefully studied, many climatic changes have taken place, apparently quite suddenly. This, according to Mr. Hapgood, is explicable if the virtually rigid outer crust of the earth undergoes, from time to time, extensive displacement . . .[3]

The consequences of a crustal displacement are monumental. As the earth's crust ripples over its interior, the world is shaken by incredible earthquakes and floods. The sky appears to fall as the crust shifts position. Day after day the sun seems to rise and set over an altered horizon, until finally the crust grinds to a halt. Beneath the ocean, earthquakes generate massive tidal waves that crash against coastlines, flooding them. Some lands are shifted to warmer climates. Others, propelled into the polar zones, suffer the direst of winters. Melting ice caps, released from the polar areas, raise the ocean's level ever higher. All living creatures must adapt, migrate, or die.

Roughly 11,600 years ago (9600 B.C.), vast climatic changes swept the planet. Massive ice sheets melted, forcing the ocean level to rise. Huge mammals perished in great numbers. There was a sudden influx of people into the Americas, and throughout the world men and women began to experiment with agriculture. Each of these critical events has become a subject of intense scientific scrutiny.

Archaeologists and anthropologists study the peopling of America and the origins of agriculture. Paleontologists, as well as anthropologists, focus on mass extinctions. Geologists ponder the movements of ice sheets. Each field proceeds with the study of "its" problems using its favourite, separate theories. Narrow specialities dominate research. But Charles Hapgood's idea offers a solution to each of these problems under the umbrella of a single event: the devastating consequences resulting when the earth's crust shifts. Through the fresh lens of Hapgood's theory, the events of 11,600 years ago are seen as the inevitable consequences of an extraordinary, but nevertheless natural, event.

Einstein's enthusiasm for Hapgood's hypothesis was fuelled by his understanding of the structure of the earth's interior. (See Illustrations 1 and 2.)

The bulk of the earth's mass lies at its centre (Illustration 1) and consists of an inner core of solid metal surrounded by an outer core of liquid metal. The outer core is encircled by the thickest part of the earth, a mantle of solid rock. Above the mantle lies the asthenosphere or "weak zone" (Illustration 2). It is the mobility of the asthenosphere that makes it possible for the earth's crust to shift.

This crust or lithosphere, which cradles the continents and ocean basins, is the thinnest layer and is the one upon which all life depends. It is divided into a series of plates that shift periodically, provoking earthquakes and volcanoes. Over millions of years, the inch-by-inch movement of these plates, explained by a theory known as "plate tectonics," can separate continents and create mountain ranges.

Plate tectonics and earth crust displacement both share the assumption of a mobile crust. The ideas are not mutually exclusive but rather complementary. Plate tectonics explains long-term, slow changes like mountain building, volcanic activity, and local earthquakes. Earth crust displacement accepts that these processes are gradual but posits a much more dramatic and abrupt movement of the crust that can explain different problems such as mass extinctions, glaciation patterns, and the sudden rise of agriculture. In stark contrast to plate tectonics' slow motion of individual plates, an "earth crust displacement," as postulated by Hapgood, abruptly shifts all the plates *as a single unit*. During this motion the core (the heavy bull's eye of the planet) doesn't change, leaving the earth's axis unaltered.

Because Hapgood's idea can be applied to so many different problems, it constitutes a "scientific revolution." In *The Structure of Scientific Revolutions*,[4] a work "commonly called the most influential

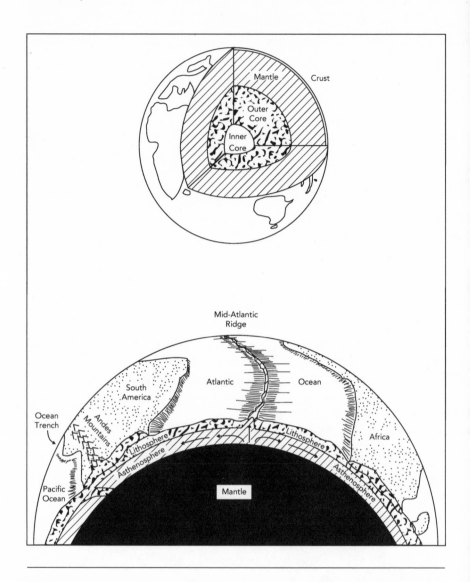

Illustrations 1 & 2: The interior of the earth consists of a series of layers. Albert Einstein endorsed Charles H. Hapgood's theory that the outer layer, the crust or lithosphere, periodically shifts over the asthenosphere. The result is catastrophic earthquakes, massive floods, and abrupt climatic change.

treatise ever written on how science does (and does not) proceed,"[5] philosopher and sociologist Thomas S. Kuhn traces the characteristics of the great changes in scientific thought. Kuhn shows how a dynamic new idea can initiate a scientific revolution by solving a set of persistent, unanswered problems. When the dust settles, intellectual territory has been expanded and scientists are presented with a fresh set of problems to explore. But ironically, the new idea that originally sparked the scientific revolution is often met with either violent controversy or smothering silence.

Darwin's theory of evolution was met with great outrage, not only by the Church, but by scientists as well. Copernicus was wise enough to have his theory published at the end of his life. He appreciated the dangers of his radical idea that the earth was not the centre of the universe. New theories are more often resisted than welcomed and indeed are often ignored, only to be recognized as scientific revolutions by a new generation. To understand this we must delve into the sociology of science.

Kuhn distinguishes between what he calls "normal science" and science in "crisis." Normal science includes activities that we commonly associate with scientific achievement, such as building a bridge, launching a space shuttle, or searching for a cure for cancer. Scientists are trained to solve problems by using well-established theories. In normal science, they make a ". . . devoted attempt to force nature into the conceptual boxes supplied by professional education."[6] Each discipline surrounds itself with a layer of insulation from problems not perceived to be within its domain. Kuhn calls these assumptions about what are "real" problems a "paradigm," a framework for approaching any scientific enigma.

Kuhn argues that the acceptance of a new framework by any scientific discipline is similar to the retooling of a factory. Initially, the costs of retooling often seem to outweigh the rewards of the improved design: "If it ain't broke don't fix it." But if the competition across town is solving more problems using the new design (the new paradigm), then all manufacturers are eventually compelled to adopt the improvements.

However, the force of competition has a less immediate impact upon science. Only when an old paradigm's blind spots are dissolved by a new idea do scientists begin to consider retooling their theories. Until this crisis occurs the old tools are wielded relentlessly, dull or outmoded as they are, even as they continue to lose their grip on the problem.

In this book, we will explore several long-standing, unsolved, and ignored problems by looking at them through the fresh lens provided by the theory of earth crust displacement. For example, an odd geological mystery surrounds today's ice sheets on Greenland and Antarctica. It is a fact that the land that holds the thickest ice sheets now receives the least annual snowfall. At the same time, the areas of thinnest ice receive the most annual snowfall. Current geological assumptions can't explain this puzzle. Only a retooling of current theory provides a grip on this phenomenon.

Likewise, several theories have been advanced to explain the terrible sudden mass extinctions of so many species in 9600 B.C. None offers as satisfactory a solution as the theory of earth crust displacement. The origins of agriculture remain a mystery and the full story behind the peopling of the Americas continues to elude the existing archaeological paradigm — and again, earth crust displacement may offer answers.

Funding also heavily influences attitudes towards new ideas. The choice of which scientific problems to pursue is seldom left to scientists themselves. They are more often than not chosen by industrial, governmental, and educational institutions. Most scientists are *assigned* to problems that seem solvable. Other problems simply receive no funding.

Moreover, the scientific community shares an implicit covenant within its ranks. Separated as it is from society, it eagerly celebrates science's success stories. Unveiling long-awaited solutions to scientific problems is a noble act. But if the general public is invited to examine a set of unsolved problems, then the scientific community becomes indignant. And indignation can rapidly lead to bitter controversy. Often a new idea is met with stony silence. That, despite the enthusiastic support of Albert Einstein, is the fate that greeted Hapgood's theory of earth crust displacement. The idea has never been disproved. There has simply been no response to it.

With one simple idea (a shifting crust), Hapgood's theory can simultaneously solve long-standing problems in geology, archaeology, anthropology, and paleontology. By opening new frontiers, this theory clears a whole new intellectual territory for scientists to explore.

Using the theory of earth crust displacement we will travel across the planet of 9600 B.C. and watch the incredible results as the surface of the earth buckles. We will explore the evidence that points to a terrible catastrophe at this time. And with it we can share the survivors' memories of a time before the flood.

We will also show that there is reason to believe that we are not the first advanced civilization to inhabit our world. This recognition provides the key to unlocking one of the most compelling mysteries of all.

The quest for Atlantis has been treated either as a scientific curiosity or with great skepticism as belonging to the murky realm of fantasy. It was inevitable that a scientific revolution would be required to find the lost continent.

•

In the mid-1960s Hapgood and his students at Keene State College began to study a series of ancient, yet amazingly accurate, maps of the globe. Strangely, the charts revealed areas of the world, such as China, North America, South America, and ice-free portions of Antarctica, long before they had been drawn by European explorers. The maps were accurate except for one crucial point: they depicted the earth as it would appear if its crust lay in a different relationship to the earth's poles than it does now. As we will see, these ancient maps represent the earth as it was *before* the last earth crust displacement, when North America was under ice and a third of Antarctica was ice-free. They show the earth as it was thousands of years ago, long before the appearance of any civilization that archaeology has yet traced.

Hapgood was convinced that only an advanced, worldwide maritime culture that existed more than ten thousand years ago could have created these maps.[7] The Greek philosopher Plato (c. 427–347 B.C.) told of a long-lost civilization that existed at this time. The legend of Atlantis was preserved by Egyptian priests for over nine thousand years. This great empire thrived on a vast island continent in a distant part of the ocean before it was destroyed by earthquakes and floods.

Plato believed that Atlantis had been created by men and women of advanced engineering skills. The capital city was also called

"Atlantis," and its layout and plan were on a gigantic scale, comparable in size to modern-day London. An immense network of canals fed the metropolis with water and carried all the necessities for survival to the citizens' front doors.

He also believed that the capital was carved from the rock of the land and arranged in a series of concentric circles. The outer ring contained a vast area devoted to traders. As one went deeper into the city one passed through gardens, racetracks, and palaces and finally arrived at the central island with its massive temple.

But the reign of the magnificent empire was destined for a violent fate.

The sky fell.

Earthquakes and floods shattered and flooded the land.

Atlantis perished.

Chapter Two Embers of Humankind

Numbed with fear, the few shocked and terrified survivors of Atlantis floated lost and confused amongst the debris left in the wake of the earth's nightmare. But the nightmare did not dissipate with the coming of the welcome dawn. There was to be no waking from this dream for many centuries. Instead it was left to those blessed by favourable winds and tides, which carried them to hospitable shores, to bind together and rebuild after the devastation.

It is a tribute to the survivors' sheer courage and overwhelming will to live that, adrift, fighting the elements, they somehow began to piece together the tattered remnants of their world. But perhaps the future could offer only hope to their battered hearts. No horror of tomorrow could compete with the devastation they had left behind, buried under the falling snow that was now smothering their island home.

But their solitude was not as total as they believed, tossed and tormented in their ships, so tiny in the ocean's vastness.

Equally as shocked as the Atlanteans were the survivors in the highlands, which had escaped the tidal waves. Shivering in their mountain-top shelters were the remaining hunters and gatherers of the earth. Clinging to the comfort of ways that had stood them well for hundreds of thousands of years, little did they suspect that those ancient routines would be overturned in a peaceful revolution, brought by strangers from the sea.

The hunters and gatherers were strong, uncoddled people, secure in the proven ways of their ancestors who had carved a living from the bounties of nature wherever they found them. They had fought the ravages of nature before: the droughts, the storms, the famines, and the thousands of dangers of chance. But nothing in their memory had been like this. Nothing had prepared them for the day the earth's crust shifted, carrying them forever away from their familiar existence. And so, shivering in their mountain retreats they began to eke out a new life in the land, until they were joined by strangers from the sea. They shared nothing with these strangers but a vivid memory of the past that had been swept away by the earth's anger and a mutual fear of the future.

We can only imagine the conflict that raged within Atlantean and non-Atlantean alike at the joy of finding other living souls. Aliens to each other they truly were: but aliens bound together by a mutual need to conquer the circumstances that threatened to destroy them all.

The first task was to secure the future with a stock of food.

Plato, who preserved the legend of Atlantis from Egyptian sources, also wrote in *Laws* about those first desperate days after the earth's convulsion as the ocean broke across its boundaries.

Athenian: Do you consider that there is any truth in the ancient tales?

Clinias: What tales?

Athenian: That the world of men has often been destroyed by floods, plagues, and many other things, in such a way that only a small portion of the human race has survived.

Clinias: Everyone would regard such accounts as perfectly credible.

Athenian: Come now, let us picture to ourselves one of the many catastrophes — namely, that which occurred once upon a time through the Deluge.

Clinias: And what are we to imagine about it?

Athenian: That the men who then escaped destruction must have been mostly herdsmen of the hill,

> scanty embers of the human race preserved
> somewhere on the mountain-tops.
>
> Clinias: Evidently . . .
>
> Athenian: Shall we assume that the cities situated in the
> plains and near the sea were totally destroyed
> at the time?
>
> Clinias: Let us assume it . . .
>
> Athenian: Shall we, then, state that, at the time when the
> destruction took place, human affairs were in
> this position: there was fearful and widespread
> desolation over a vast tract of land; most of the
> animals were destroyed; and the few herds of
> oxen and flocks of goats that happened to
> survive afforded at the first but scanty
> sustenance to their herdsmen? . . .[1]

Plato's account represents the earliest rational explanation for the appearance of domesticated animals. His theory postulates the emergence of agriculture, beginning with the domestication of animals, as a reappearance of a skill learned long before, in Atlantis. As we will see, the dating of the earliest experiments with agriculture appears to match the century of Atlantis's fall.

Plato's vision is also remarkable for the fact that it presents a physical, rather than a mythological, cause of agriculture. Before his time, all explanations relied upon the intervention of gods and goddesses to account for the beginning of agriculture:

> In the classical mythologies of all civilizations, agriculture
> is fundamentally of divine origin. It arrived in different
> ways from different deities and under various circum-
> stances, but the underlying theme is recognizable.[2]

In contrast to these mythological origins of agriculture, Plato presents a very different picture. In his view, agriculture *re-emerges* after the destruction of a great and advanced civilization by "earth-quakes and floods of extraordinary violence." There are no gods or goddesses to suddenly intervene in the affairs of humankind. In-stead, Plato sees the emergence of agriculture as a long, slow battle to recover the foundations of a lost civilization. His is a vision of human beings struggling against the vastly transformed physical conditions brought in the wake of the Great Flood.

We have travelled eons in our methods of farming since those first desperate days and in the process have become dependent upon a few key crops and domesticated animals. In North America, the great "bread basket of the world," a small fraction of the population toils to harvest the crops. The efforts of these few and their highly specialized equipment have transformed the landscape. To create more and more fertile plants we intervene in the reproductive process of many crops such as wheat, rice, and corn — crops that would soon be swallowed by wild grasses if left to fend for themselves.

Mile after mile of domestic grains, bent to humankind's design, have replaced towering prairie grasses. From the transformed American prairie to the African savannah and Brazilian jungle, wild vegetation has submitted to the demands of the plow. Squeezed by overpopulation, we continuously strip away the natural garment of the earth and cover it with a cloth of our own weave. Our reliance upon agriculture is complete. We can't turn back.

The modern search for the origins of agriculture has been one of archaeology's most persistent quests. Numerous theories have attempted to explain the sudden rise of agriculture on different continents following the climatic changes of 9600 B.C. In 1886, Alphonse de Candolle (1806–93) took a botanical approach to the problem:

> One of the most direct means of discovering the geographic origin of a cultivated species, is to seek in what country it grows spontaneously, and without the help of man.[3]

A dedicated Soviet botanist, Nikolai Ivanovich Vavilov (1887–1943), saw the possibilities in de Candolle's approach. Vavilov eventually gathered a collection of over fifty thousand wild plants from around the globe. In doing so he ". . . located EIGHT INDEPENDENT CENTERS OF ORIGIN of the world's most important cultivated plants"[4] and identified a direct relationship between the eight centres and the earth's highest mountain ranges.

It is clear that the zone of initial development of the most important cultivated plants lies in the strip between 20 and 45° north latitude, near the high mountain ranges, the Himalayas, the Hindu Kush, those of the Near East, the Balkans, and the Apennines. In the Old World this strip follows the latitudes while in the New World it runs longitudinally, in both cases conforming to the general direction of the great mountain ranges.[5]

(See Maps 1a and 1b.)

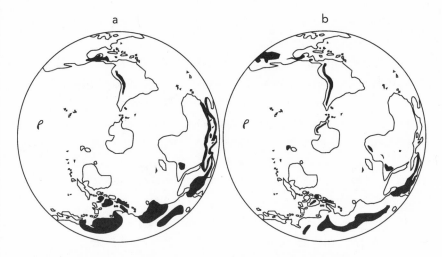

Agricultural origins altitude: a) Vavilov's eight centres of agricultural origins; and b) land over 1,500 metres above sea level.

Maps 1a & b: When we place Antarctica at the centre of a world map we can see the sites where agriculture originated according to the Russian botanist Nikolai Vavilov. Most domesticated plants and animals were originally domesticated in centres 1,500 metres above ocean level. Agriculture was reborn in these mountains 11,600 years ago. Survivors of the Great Flood were terrified of descending to the lowlands in case another earthquake would cause floods to destroy their world. Only after many generations were the survivors brave enough to bring their plants and animals from the highlands to lower elevations. The earliest civilizations were often found downriver from high mountains.

Vavilov proved that most of the world's domesticated crops were derived from plants that originated in mountains high above sea level. His results, unwittingly, supported Plato's claim of the importance of highlands to agricultural origins.[6]

Plato dates the origins of agriculture to approximately 9600 B.C. when the earth shook and a great civilization was destroyed. How did Plato, so long ago, accurately identify the time of these developments? A time that modern archaeologists only established after the Second World War?[7] After all, he was without the benefit of radiocarbon dating.

He claimed that his knowledge of the events, which occurred during and after the Great Flood, came from an Egyptian priest who had access to the written records of the lost island continent of Atlantis.[8]

If Plato is right, we aren't the first world culture to become ensnared in a dependency upon the more advanced processes of agriculture. According to Plato, the Atlanteans constructed elaborate canals to irrigate immense areas for cultivation. They, too, were accomplished farmers. But when the end came, only a few possessed the necessary skills to select the wild plants in the new lands that would be suitable to ensure a regular crop. Those few would be enough.

The survivors of the Great Flood, terrified at the prospect of being swept away by another deluge, settled at higher altitudes where they could remain in safety, nurturing their ancient skills, including agriculture. When they finally descended from the highlands to settle on the plains, they may have been regarded as superhuman by the half-starved local populations. The Atlanteans now ruled over the ruins of a world humbled by the earth's "fearful and widespread desolation."

The last Atlanteans found themselves stripped of their homeland, their past destroyed, and their future bleak as they faced their only escape route — the open sea. Where could they go? Their limited choice was dictated by the overwhelming climatic changes that had been forced over the planet. As the crust shifted, some lands became warmer as they moved towards the equator and others became colder, shoved closer to the icy polar regions. Some areas escaped climatic change, while the climate of others actually improved.

The world was in climatic upheaval. Survivors from the lost land had to make their way through the rubble. They had to find those areas of the globe that offered refuge from the ravages of climatic transformation and a rising ocean. They sought out the highlands, but not all highlands could offer safety. Three areas in the world's tropics offered climatic stability and highlands to settle. They were each midway between the former and current path of the equator. They each received the same amount of annual sunlight before and after the earth crust displacement. These sites proved to be the most important places in the origins of tropical agriculture. All were over 1,500 metres above sea level and in areas that lay between the former and current path of the equator (see Map 2).

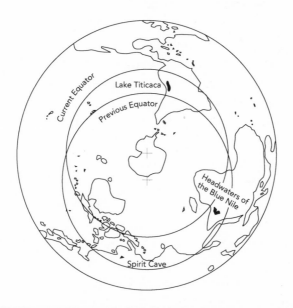

Map 2: Seen from Antarctica, the path of the equator shifted with the last earth crust displacement. Lake Titicaca in the central Andes, Spirit Cave located in the highlands of Thailand, and the highlands of Ethiopia were all midway between the current and former path of the equator. These favourable sites were climatically stable and supplied the survivors with raw crops that became potatoes, rice, and millet. The earliest agricultural sites date to 9600 B.C., the same time that Plato says Atlantis perished.

Agriculture was coaxed to life again in South America near Lake Titicaca. In this single place in the Americas, plants and animals did not have to migrate in order to survive. The annual sunshine remained the same as before the earth crust displacement. Here the first potatoes were domesticated and llamas and guinea pigs were bred. Here the survivors of Atlantis might rebuild their civilization high above the ocean and free of the fear of tidal waves. Here there was hope.[9]

On the opposite side of the globe, rice was domesticated at Spirit Cave in the highlands of Thailand shortly after the displacement (see Map 2). The origins of tropical agriculture in South America and Southeast Asia occurred at approximately the same time on exactly opposite sides of the globe, an archaeological phenomenon explained by the earth crust displacement theory, which pinpoints these two places as areas of stability after the climatic upheaval of 9600 B.C.[10]

After hundreds of thousands of years of living by hunting and gathering, humankind turned to experimenting with agriculture on opposite sides of the earth at the same time. Is this likely without the intervention of some outside force? Was that force from a lost paradise in Antarctica?

Africa suffered fewer latitude changes than the other continents. In the Ethiopian highlands, around the headwaters of the Blue Nile, the amount of annual sunshine was unaltered after the last earth crust displacement. Because it was roughly the same distance from the equator after the catastrophe as before, it became an oasis of survival. The highlands of Ethiopia may yet yield surprises for archaeologists. Here millet was first domesticated. These highlands would have been an excellent site for the survivors of Atlantis to settle because here, as in Lake Titicaca, the climate was not dramatically changed as a result of the earth crust displacement. Atlanteans may have survived here and eventually followed the Blue Nile down to Egypt to participate in the development of the Egyptian civilization.

Egypt was one of the world's earliest known civilizations. It shared with Crete, Sumeria, India, and China a common fate after the last earth crust displacement. Each of these cultures emerged in an area that, although tropical before the displacement, became temperate after.[11] Plants and animals already adapted to a temperate climate could migrate into this new temperate area. Grasslands flourished. Animals followed. The land thrived. Here sheep, pigs, goats, and cattle were all first brought under the yolk of domestication. Here also two of the world's most important crops — wheat and barley — were shaped to humans' design. This great crescent of land, extending from Egypt to Japan, adjoined an area to the north that remained temperate both before and after the displacement. (See Map 3.)

Could it be mere coincidence that the first five known civilizations should all share a common climatic fate?

Map 3: A vast crescent of land extending from Egypt to Japan was tropical before the earth crust displacement and temperate afterwards. This favoured crescent was the birthplace of the world's first known civilizations.

The theory of earth crust displacement imposes an order on the mystery behind the sudden, global emergence of agriculture shortly after 9600 B.C. The same theory, that the earth's crust is sometimes radically displaced, can explain the peopling of the Americas and the puzzling glaciation patterns found in both hemispheres. This was the idea Albert Einstein claimed was ". . . of great importance to everything that is related to the history of the earth's surface."

Parts of humanity's history have been destroyed by the volatility of the earth's crust, severing our link to the past. But some of the chain might be repaired if we listen carefully to a recurring myth whispered around campfires across the globe. The myth, although told about different characters and using various literary devices, always depicts the same sequence: the sky falls (or the sun wavers) and a great flood engulfs the world. Survivors begin a new era.

Chapter Three

The Wayward Sun

I t is sunset at the camp of the tribe known as the Utes. Preparations for the annual Sun-Dance have begun. Men and women draped in rabbit-skin robes are drawn to the fire's glow. Dishes of simmering turtle, lizard, insects, and generous servings of berries and seeds are shared around the circle. It is time. An elder rises and passes a lined hand over his buffalo-skin cloak. The children are immediately alert, their eyes wide with anticipation.

Listen now, on this feast of the Sun-Dance, to the Utes' myth of the taming of the sun-god:

> Once upon a time Ta-wats, the hare-god, was sitting with his family by the camp-fire in the solemn woods, anxiously waiting for the return of Ta-vi, the wayward sun-god. Wearied with long watching, the hare-god fell asleep, and the sun-god came so near that he scorched the naked shoulder of Ta-wats. Foreseeing the vengeance which would be thus provoked, he fled back to his cave beneath the earth.
>
> Ta-wats awoke in great anger, and speedily determined to go and fight the sun-god. After a long journey of many adventures the hare-god came to the brink of the earth, and there watched long and patiently, till at last the sun-god coming out he shot an arrow at his face, but the fierce heat consumed the arrow ere it had finished its intended course; then another was sped, but that also was consumed; and another, and still another, till only one

remained in his quiver, but this was the magical arrow that had never failed its mark.

Ta-wats, holding it in his hand, lifted the barb to his eye and baptized it in a divine tear; then the arrow was sped and struck the sun-god full in the face, and the sun was shivered into a thousand fragments which fell to the earth, causing a general conflagration.

Then Ta-wats, the hare-god, fled before the destruction he had wrought, and as he fled the burning earth consumed his feet, consumed his legs, consumed his body, consumed his hands and his arms — all were consumed but the head alone, which bowled across valleys and over mountains, fleeing the destruction from the burning earth, until at last, swollen with heat, the eyes of the god burst and the tears gushed forth in a flood which spread over the earth and extinguished the fire.

The sun-god was now conquered, and he appeared before a council of the gods to await sentence. In that long council were established the days and the nights, the seasons and the years, with the length thereof, and the sun was condemned to travel across the firmament by the same trail day after day till the end of time.[1]

The Utes, after whom Utah was named, were among the most warlike tribes in the American West. They fought with the Comanche, Arapaho, Kiowa, and Cheyenne for domination over hunting grounds. Young braves were taught when to attack, when to retreat, and when to find honour in vengeance. These challenges were interwoven with forceful lessons about the humbling power of nature. Tales of the hare-god's antics and the sun-god's power were much more than exciting children's stories. The myths illustrated the critical factors a warrior must weigh in times of battle: how the seasons came to be, and why the sun follows its predictable path across the sky. This cohesive view of the world was strong glue binding the tribe together.

The myth was also a reflection of the human need to create order out of nature's chaos. The social problems of war and peace were mirrored in nature's forces of chaos and order. Ta-wats, the hare-god, is sleeping in the woods when the wayward sun provokes him by scorching his shoulder. He rises and seeks revenge upon the fleeing sun-god. Eventually the sun-god is attacked with a magic arrow and the explosive forces of nature are released. The sun erupts and a great flood engulfs the world. Order is restored only when a council of the gods creates predictable seasons and condemns the sun to follow an unalterable path across the heavens until "the end of time."

The myth of the wayward sun can also be seen as a distant echo of the last earth crust displacement. As the ground shuddered beneath them it would have seemed to its shocked inhabitants that the sky, sun, and stars were tumbling from their place in the heavens. The violent earthquakes caused by the displacement generated great tidal waves that rolled across the ocean, smashing vulnerable coastlines. Ice caps melted, forcing the ocean level higher and higher. For many it was the end of the world. But for the survivors, it became the first day of a new world order.

The German-American anthropologist Franz Boas (1858–1942) traced the mythology of the Utes to the Canadian province of British Columbia,[2] where the mythological trail connected the Utes with the Kutenai, and in turn the Okanagan. The Kutenai occupy territory encompassing parts of British Columbia, Alberta, Washington, Idaho, and Montana. Like the Utes, the Kutenai speak of a great fire that erupted over the earth when the sun was struck by an arrow: "Coyote is envious, and shoots the sun at sunrise. His arrows catch fire, fall down, and set fire to the grass."[3]

And the Kutenai speak of the fear they have that the world will come to an end when the sky loses its stability: "The Kutenai look for Polaris [the North Star] every night. Should it not be in place, the end of the world is imminent."[4]

Little is known of the origin of the Kutenai.[5] They often have wavy hair, light brown skin, and slight beards.[6] Their neighbours in the plains, the Blackfoot, gave them the name Kutenai, which is a Blackfoot word for "white men."[7] Franz Boas believed that the Kutenai were mythologically linked with their neighbours to the west, the Okanagan.[8] The Okanagan called the Kutenai by the name "skelsa'ulk," which has been translated as the "water people."[9]

In 1886, the famous American historian Hubert Howe Bancroft (1832–1918) related the Okanagan myth of their lost island paradise of "Samah-tumi-whoo-lah":

> Long, long ago, when the sun was young and no bigger than a star, there was an island far off in the middle of the ocean. It was called Samah-tumi-whoo-lah, meaning White Man's Island. On it lived a race of giants — white giants. Their ruler was a tall white woman called Scomalt . . . She could create whatever she wished.
>
> For many years the white giants lived at peace, but at last they quarreled amongst themselves. Quarreling grew into war. The noise of battle was heard, and many people were killed. Scomalt was made very, very angry . . . she drove the wicked giants to one end of White Man's Island. When they were gathered together in one place, she broke off that piece of land and pushed it out to sea. For many days the floating island drifted on the water, tossed by waves and wind. All the people on it died except one man and one woman.
>
> . . . Seeing that their island was about to sink they built a canoe [and] . . . after paddling for many days and nights, they came to some islands. They steered their way through them and at last reached the mainland.[10]

The Okanagan and the Utes feared any dramatic change in the heavens as an ominous portent of another Great Flood. The fear that the sun might once again wander or the sky might fall became an obsession. The Utes related that: "Some think the sky is supported by one big cottonwood tree in the west and another in the east; if either get rotten, it may break and the sky would fall down, killing everybody."[11]

And the Okanagan believed that in a time to come,

> . . . [the] lakes will melt the foundations of the world, and the rivers will cut the world loose. Then it will float as the island did many suns and snows ago. That will be the end of the world.[12]

As we move south we encounter the Washo of western Nevada who are famous for their decorative basketry. They lived on the eastern flank of the Sierra Nevada Mountains. The tribe was always small, never overhunting the earth. They ranged from a population of 900 in 1859 to just over 800 in 1980. In earlier times, their numbers may have reached 1,500.[13] They were a solitary people who told a tale of a time, long, long ago, when the mountains shook with volcanoes and "so great was the heat of the blazing mountains that the very stars melted and fell."[14]

Along the Gila and Salt River valleys of Arizona live the remnants of the A'a'tam tribe, who have been misnamed by outsiders not once, but twice. Because an Italian explorer sailing under the Spanish flag in 1492 didn't know where he was, the entire native population of the Americas was christened, wrongly, "Indians." And when the early missionaries demanded that the A'a'tam tribe identify themselves they refused, answering in their native tongue with the single word, "pima," meaning "no." From this exchange a misunderstanding arose that remains to this day. The missionaries took the "pima" response as an answer to their question rather than a refusal to cooperate, and so the tribe came to be known as the Pima.[15]

In fact, "A'a'tam" means "people."

Part of the A'a'tam's history was carried across the centuries in an age-old myth of a great flood that had once overwhelmed the earth. Their tale of the flood included an event absent from the frontiersmen's Bible. Using the symbolism of a magical baby created by an evil deity, the myth told how the screaming child "shook the earth," catapulting the world into the horrors of the great flood.[16]

The A'a'tam now feared that the sky was insecure. Corrective measures were called for and the Earth Doctor created a grey spider that spun a huge web around the edges of the sky and earth to hold them secure. But still the fear remained that the fragile web might break, releasing the sky and causing the earth to tremble.[17]

In 1849, the California Gold Rush brought white men streaming across the Rocky Mountains to the west coast, home of the Cahto. Ten years later, the pioneers of Mendocina County in northwestern California killed thirty-two Cahto because they took some livestock belonging to the whites. These thirty-two men represented more than 6 percent of the Cahto's population. To put this tragedy in perspective, we can imagine the havoc wreaked on the United States today if the populations of New York City, Chicago, and Los Angeles were suddenly murdered by some alien force. The Cahto never recovered. By 1910, 90 percent of the population was dead.

The mythology of this lost culture stretched back nearly twelve thousand years to the time of the last earth crust displacement. Through this legacy we learn of the catapulting events in California at the time of the Great Flood: "The sky fell. The land was not. For a very great distance there was no land. The waters of the ocean came together. Animals of all kinds drowned."[18]

American native mythology identifies four westerly mountains tied to the aftermath of a great flood. All four lie immediately west of land, and each is 1,800 metres or higher above sea level. At the time of the Great Flood, this land would have been the first hope for those survivors of the lost island paradise who had travelled so far across an endless ocean (see Map 4).

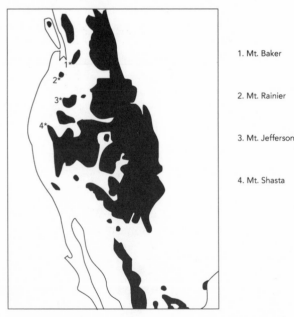

1. Mt. Baker

2. Mt. Rainier

3. Mt. Jefferson

4. Mt. Shasta

Map 4: Native myths honour four mountains as sites of ancestral survival after the Great Flood. These sites suggest the ancestors arrived from the Pacific Ocean.

The native people of Washington and Oregon claim that their ancestors came in great canoes and landed on Mount Baker[19] and Mount Jefferson.[20] They believed that Mount Rainier[21] was the refuge of those who were saved after the wicked of the earth were destroyed in a great flood. The Shasta of northern California tell of a time when the sun fell from its normal course.[22] In a separate myth they tell how Mount Shasta saved their ancestors from the Deluge.[23]

●

On the opposite side of North America lies another great mountain chain, the Appalachians. Here also, tales were told of terrifying solar changes, massive floods, and the survivors of these catastrophes.

The lush green forests of the southern tip of the Appalachian Mountains were once the home of the Cherokee. In the early part of the nineteenth century, a Cherokee named Sequoya created an alphabet for writing the tribal language. His work left a rich legacy of myths transcribed from his people's oral tradition. In one of these myths, the flood is attributed to the uncontrollable tears of the sun-goddess.

It was said that she hated people and cursed them with a great drought. In desperation the Cherokee elders consulted "Little Men" (whom they regarded as gods). They decreed that the Cherokees' only hope of survival was to *kill the sun*. Magical snakes were prepared to deal a death blow to the sun-goddess. But a tragic mistake was made and her daughter, the moon, was struck instead:

> When the Sun found her daughter dead, she went into the house and grieved, and the people did not die any more, but now the world was dark all the time, because the Sun would not come out.
>
> They went again to the Little Men, and told them if they wanted the Sun to come out again they must bring back her daughter . . . [Seven men went to the ghost country and retrieved the moon but on the return journey she died again. The sun-goddess cried and wept . . .] until *her tears made a flood upon the earth*, and the people were afraid the world would be drowned. (italics added)[24]

The Cherokee, like the Utes and Okanagan tribes, had a dark prophecy of how the world would end:

> The earth is a great island floating in a sea of water, and suspended at each of the four cardinal points by a cord hanging down from the sky vault, which is of solid rock. When the world grows old and worn out, the people will die and the cords will break and let the earth sink into the ocean, and all will be water *again*. (italics added)[25]

Despite the fact that they both lived in mountain ranges, far from the ocean, the Cherokee and Okanagan people associated the mythological flood with an island. For the Okanagan this island lay "far off in the middle of the ocean." For the Cherokee, the myth of the "great island floating in a sea" contains clues to this lost land: "There is another world under this, and it is like ours in every-thing — animals, plants, and people — save that the seasons are different."[26]

There is, in fact, just such an island in the middle of the ocean with a climate opposite to that of the northern hemisphere. The island continent of Antarctica was partially ice-free before the last earth crust displacement (see Map 5). Was it the drowned island of Okanagan/Cherokee mythology?

The people of Central America hold a rich mythology about the lost island paradise and its destruction in a great flood. We will explore their legacy later.

The people of South America also tell myths of a flood and of the events surrounding it. The Ipurinas of northwestern Brazil retain one of the most elegant myths about the disaster: ". . . long ago the Earth was overwhelmed by a hot flood. This took place when the sun, a cauldron of boiling water, tipped over."[27]

Further south, after their sweeping victories in Mexico and Peru, the Spanish conquistadors assumed that Chile would be another easy target. Santiago, the Spanish capital, was founded in February 1541 by Pedro de Valdiva, the first Spanish governor. Six months later the city was destroyed by the native people of Chile, the Araucanians, who launched a war that continued for four centuries.

Map 5: Antarctica is an island in the middle of the ocean, just like the lost land of Okanagan mythology. And like the floating disc of Cherokee mythology, Lesser Antarctica would have experienced seasons opposite to those of North America. It may have been, before the last earth crust displacement, the lost island paradise of native American mythology.

Here was a tribe so valiant that they would fight for generations rather than submit to slavery. But even these brave people trembled before a traumatic memory: "The Flood was the result of a volcanic eruption accompanied by a violent earthquake, and whenever there is an earthquake the natives rush to the high mountains. They are afraid that after the earthquake the sea may again drown the world."[28]

Like the Araucanians, the Inca were paralyzed by the fear that any change in the sun foretold doom. A 1555 Spanish chronicle spoke of this trepidation: ". . . [when] there is an eclipse of the sun or the moon the Indians cry and groan in great perturbation, thinking that the time has come in which the earth will perish . . ."[29]

●

The famous Peruvian historian, Garcilasso de la Vega, son of a Spanish conquistador and an Inca princess, asked his Inca uncle to tell him the story of his people's origins. How had Lake Titicaca become the source of their civilization? The uncle explained:

> . . . in ancient times all this region which you see was covered with forests and thickets, and the people lived like brute beasts without religion nor government, nor towns, nor houses, without cultivating the land nor covering their bodies . . . [the sun-god sent a son and daughter to] . . . give them precepts and laws by which to live as reasonable and civilized men, and to teach them to dwell in houses and towns, to cultivate maize and other crops, to breed flocks, and to use the fruits of the earth as rational beings . . .[30]

The "gods" who brought agriculture to the vicinity of Lake Titicaca were said to have come "out of the regions of the south"[31] immediately "after the deluge."[32] In other words, agriculture was introduced to Lake Titicaca by people who already possessed the skill but had been forced to leave their homeland when a flood destroyed their southern land.

The word "Inca" means "Son of the Sun" and was a title originally carried only by the Emperor. To preserve his culture from the ravages of the conquistadors, Inca Manco II left the great capital of Cuzco in 1536 and retreated into the daunting heights of the Andes. He took with him three sons, each of whom would, in turn, become Inca and suffer a succession of bloody encounters with the Spanish. Manco II chose a mountain peak overlooking the Urubamba valley to build his palace. Pizarro, leader of the Spanish invaders, was never able to find this secret base and its existence intrigued those who followed him. All who tried to discover the lost city failed.

Later, in the same century, two monks, Friar Marcos and Friar Diego, did come tantalizingly close to lifting the veil of the hidden city. Friar Marcos was fired with a ". . . desire to seek souls where not a single preacher had entered and where the gospel message had not been heard."[33] Travelling with him was a medical missionary, Friar Diego, who became popular with the local people and a favourite of the royal Inca. The two monks had established a convent at Puquiura, near Vitcos, and were fascinated by Inca stories of the "Virgins of the Sun" who dwelt in a fabulous city known as "Vilcabamba the Old." This city in the mountains was said to house great "wizards and masters of abomination."[34]

Daily, the two monks tried to coax the Inca, who didn't always remain in the hidden city, into revealing the location of his city. Finally, he agreed to take them. Higher and higher they travelled, the air becoming thinner with every step. The Inca was carried in a litter and enjoyed the view while the monks stumbled through the thick jungle, their clumsy robes entangling their every step. After three days they arrived at the foot of yet another barrier of mountains that jutted even further into the sky.

For three weeks the monks preached and taught the natives who lived in a settlement just beyond sight and sound of the mystery city. They were forbidden to enter its enclaves for fear they would learn something of its rites, ceremonies, and purpose. During the night, the Inca priests high in the forbidden city conspired to corrupt the monks by sending beautiful women to tempt them from their vows of celibacy. Friars Marcos and Diego resisted to the end and finally concluded that they would never reach the sacred city. It was never found by the Spanish.

In 1911, four centuries later, the American historian and explorer Hiram Bingham (1875–1956) discovered the marvellous, haunting ruins of a lost Inca city cradled in the summit of a mountain called Machu Picchu. He believed that he had discovered the lost city of "Vilcabamba the Old" where the "Virgins of the Sun" catered to the wishes of their Inca master.[35] He recovered a number of skeletons from Machu Picchu, which he sent to Dr. George Eaton of Yale University. The professor concluded that among the skeletons:

> . . . there was not a single one of a robust male of the warrior type. There are a few effeminate males who might very well have been priests, but the large majority of the skeletons are female . . .[36]

Why did the Inca retain a settlement of young women in this mountain retreat, Machu Picchu?

A clue might come from the U.S. Air Force and its bunker buried deep beneath Colorado Springs. It was built as a retreat in the event of nuclear war and a base from which to re-establish civilization. For the Inca, the threat was not nuclear but rather a great flood. To meet this threat, they created bases on mountains far from the ocean. If another deluge were unleashed, a base like Machu Picchu could repopulate a drowned world.

In his book, *The Lost City of the Incas*, Bingham described one of the rituals performed at each winter solstice by the priests of Machu Picchu.[37] A mystical cord was secured by a great stone pillar to "guide" the sun across the sky, preventing it from losing course.

This "Intihuatana" or "hitching post of the sun" may have been a ritualistic attempt to prevent another earth crust displacement. If so, then the mysterious appearance of solar megaliths (known as Sun Stones) around the globe may have represented ancient attempts to secure the sun in its new path across the sky after the Flood. A reined sun could not release another great flood. The earth would be safe for another year.

This obsession with the stability of the sun's path is found in the American southwest among the ruins of the Anasazi (a Navajo word meaning "the ancient ones"). They are famed for their cliff dwellings, their circular architecture, and other artistic achievements. Chaco Mesa in New Mexico is the site of one of the most remarkable solar megaliths in the world. Three slabs of stone, each weighing two tons, have been arranged so that the light of the sun falls on a spiral petroglyph marking the summer and winter solstices and the spring and fall equinoxes (see Illustration 3).

Discovered in 1977 by artist and amateur archaeo-astronomer Anna Sofaer,[38] this solar calendar has been called a "sun dagger" because of the pattern the sunlight makes on the rock carvings during the summer solstice. Sofaer called the marking a "sun dagger" but it may have actually served as the Anasazi's equivalent of the Incas' hitching post of the sun. If so, it would be more properly called a "solar cord," designed to prevent a wayward sun or at least

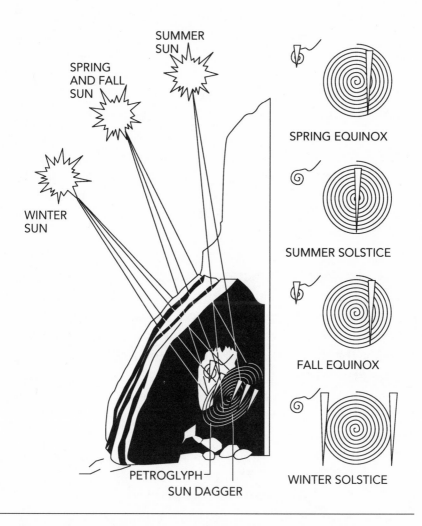

Illustration 3: In Chaco Mesa, New Mexico, the Anasazi may have attached a "solar cord" to large stones during each summer solstice. Ensuring the safety of the sun's movements was a worldwide obsession after the last earth crust displacement.

monitor the sun's path to ensure that all was in order. The fear of a wayward sun or falling sky became a global nightmare for the survivors of the last earth crust displacement.

For example, from 400 to 1200 A.D. the Celts occupied much of central and western Europe. They were known as fearless warriors who " . . . did not dread earthquakes or high tides, which, indeed, they attacked with weapons; but they feared the fall of the sky and the day when fire and water must prevail."[39]

And in 1643, a bishop in Iceland discovered a very ancient manuscript containing the most detailed information ever found about Germanic myths. These myths open with the haunting prophecy of an inspired seeress: "The sun turns black, earth sinks into the sea, The hot stars down from the heaven are whirled . . ."[40]

The overwhelming anxiety that earthquakes might foreshadow a worldwide flood was suffered not just by those who dwelled on the lip of the ocean. The Mari, who still occupy the land west of the Volga River in Russia, believed that the earth was supported on one horn (the other had broken before the Great Flood) of a massive bull. The bull, in turn, balanced precariously on the back of a giant crab, which crouched on the ocean floor. Any movement of the bull's head was thought to cause earthquakes. The Mari lived in terror that the bull's remaining horn would snap, sending the earth tumbling once more into the ocean. As the beast's head tipped, throwing the earth forward, violent earthquakes would erupt. And then, as the earth was pitched from the bull's single horn and hurtled through the air, the sky would seem to fall. Finally, the earth would tumble into the ocean, releasing a cataclysm of water that would drown the world.[41]

Throughout ancient Europe giant stones were erected to honour the sun. Stonehenge in Wiltshire, England, is one of the most famous of these sites. Like the structures in North and South America, Stonehenge may have been built as a magical device designed to prevent another earth crust displacement. By controlling the sun's movements, these massive stones might ensure the safety of the world.

The horseshoe mouth of the stones is open to receive the sun's rays on the summer solstice. The body of the horseshoe corresponds to the path of the sun from sunrise to sunset. Each day, as spring moves towards summer, the sun rises slightly farther north on the morning horizon. On the summer solstice this "migration" north seems to stall. The day after the solstice, the sun reverses its journey and begins to rise farther south each morning. To a people ever vigilant to the dangers of a wayward sun, any irregularity threatens catastrophe. To prevent this, the priests may have, like their counterparts on Machu Picchu, attempted to "harness" the sun by "tying" its rays to successive stones within the horseshoe. The world would be safe for another year.

In Egypt, the pyramids were also precisely aligned with the rising sun on the summer solstice. In an ancient Egyptian writing the sun-god decrees: "I am the one who hath made the water which becomes the Great Flood . . ."[42] The sun "is usually said to have been born on or by 'the great flood.'"[43]

In Egyptian mythology, the world was seen as a bubble within an endless "Primordial Abyss of Waters":

> This was unlike any sea which has a surface, for here there was neither up nor down, no distinction of side, only a limitless deep — endless, dark, and infinite. . . . it was thought that the seas, the rivers, the rain from heaven, and the waters in the wells, and the torrents of the floods were parts of the Primeval Waters which enveloped the world on every side.[44]

The Egyptians feared that these Primeval Waters might eventually seep into the world, flooding it. The pyramids, artificial mountains aligned with the "new" path of the sun, may symbolize the mountain upon which the survivors of the last Great Flood ultimately found refuge.[45] The builders of these ancient monuments may have been paying homage to the land that their ancestors clung to after the Flood.

From all corners of the Earth, the same story is told. The sun deviates from its regular path. The sky falls. The earth is wrenched and torn by earthquakes. And finally a great wave of water engulfs the globe. Survivors of such a calamity would go to any lengths to prevent it from happening again. They lived in an age of magic. It was natural and necessary to construct elaborate devices to pacify the sun-god (or goddess) and control or monitor its path.

Is it any wonder that so many ancient people have called themselves "Children of the Sun"? It was perhaps only later that this label became one of pride. At first it may well have been a frantic appease-ment to the violent sun-god. The sun was feared, the sky untethered, and the ocean volatile. A wayward sun might initiate a chain of events that could brutally shatter our world.

But why did the sky fall?

Chapter Four

Why the Sky Fell

In the summer of 1799, while searching for ivory in the isolated wilderness of Siberia, a Tungus chief named Ossip Shumakhov encountered, complete with preserved hair and flesh, the ice-encapsulated carcass of a mammoth. The chief was terrified. Legend foretold that any whose gaze fell upon one of these creatures would soon die. As predicted, within a few days Ossip grew ill. However, to his own and everyone else's surprise, he made a complete recovery.

With renewed courage, Ossip set out to revisit the frozen mammoth, this time taking along several curious Russian scientists. Excited to discover that Ossip's fantastic account was true, they shipped the remains of the incredible creature to St. Petersburg, where it can still be seen today.

On the heels of this sensational discovery, the New Siberian Islands, in the Arctic Ocean, gave up the desolate graves of thousands of large animals. The find created confusion among scientists. How could these huge creatures, requiring vast amounts of vegetation to fuel their daily existence, thrive in such large herds on barren dunes of ice? And what incredible force had destroyed them?

One of the first and most distinguished scholars to accept the challenge of these questions was Georges Cuvier (1769–1832), a French naturalist. Cuvier had already created a sensation by unearthing and reassembling a prehistoric elephant from the ground beneath Paris. This was only one of the amazing discoveries that the inquisitive Monsieur Cuvier would reveal to a startled Europe. By his mid-thirties he had become the dominant scientific thinker of his era, clearing new paths in virtually all of the natural sciences.

The naturalist's flamboyant character, combined with his colourful discoveries, made him a favourite object of popular gossip. One story was repeated again and again in the fashionable salons. It was said that late one night, Cuvier's students decided to play a practical joke on him. One, dressed in a red cape to represent the Devil, artificial horns secured to his head, and hooves tied to his feet, burst into the sleeping professor's chambers shouting that he had come to devour the learned scientist!

Cuvier pulled himself up and, leaning on one elbow, calmly examined the spectacle before him. He then announced, "You have horns and hooves; you can only eat plants!"

In his meticulously organized laboratory, to which only a few were admitted, Cuvier laboured long hours over the mystery of the ancient bones from Siberia and the inevitable questions they raised. He became more and more convinced that the world had experienced a catastrophe of unspeakable dimensions and that man:

> . . . might have inhabited certain circumscribed regions, whence he repeopled the earth after these terrible events; perhaps even the places he inhabited were entirely swallowed up and his bones buried in the depths of the present seas, except for a small number of individuals who carried on the race.[1]

The unexpected discovery of frozen giants in the wastelands of Siberia excited Cuvier's genius and proved to him that the earth had suffered sudden, destructive convulsions and upheavals:

> These repeated irruptions and retreats of the sea have neither been slow nor gradual; most of the catastrophes which have occasioned them have been sudden; and this is easily proved, especially with regard to the last of them, the traces of which are most conspicuous. In the northern regions it has left the carcasses of some large quadrupeds which the ice had arrested, and which are preserved even to the present day with their skin, their hair, and their flesh. If they had not been frozen as soon as killed they must quickly have been decomposed by putrefaction. But

this eternal frost could not have taken possession of the regions which these animals inhabited except by the same cause which destroyed them; this cause, therefore, must have been as sudden as its effect. The breaking to pieces and overturnings of the strata, which happened in former catastrophes, shew [sic] plainly enough that they were sudden and violent like the last; and the heaps of debris and rounded pebbles which are found in various places among the solid strata, demonstrate the vast force of the motions excited in the mass of waters by these overturnings. Life, therefore, has been often disturbed on this earth by terrible events — calamities which, at their commencement, have perhaps moved and *overturned to a great depth the entire outer crust of the globe*, but which, since these first commotions, have uniformly acted at a less depth and less generally. (italics added)[2]

At the time Cuvier put forth his theory, geologists were involved in an intense debate with the Church over the role of catastrophes in the earth's history. Although he was greatly respected, Cuvier's theory of an earth crust displacement was unacceptable to the scientific establishment. It was associated with the idea of a supernatural force (God) that could overturn the laws of nature at will. It was also unacceptable to the religious fanatics, who, although they liked Cuvier's earthquakes and floods, didn't accept his timing, which placed these events far earlier than the Bible did. And so Cuvier's theory that mass extinctions were caused by displacements of the earth's crust was suffocated in the heated debate between religious fanatics and defensive scientists.

However, one man based his studies on Cuvier's theory, giving us what is still an accepted notion: the Ice Ages. Naturalist and geologist Louis Agassiz (1807–73) was born in Môtier, Switzerland. From an early age Agassiz was blessed with the ambition and determination to make his unique mark upon the history of science. Only twenty-two when his first work, *Brazilian Fish*, was published, he dedicated the book to Georges Cuvier, "whom I revere as a father, and whose works have been till now my only guide." Cuvier responded to the young scientist with a complimentary letter suggesting additional lines of investigation.

With this encouragement, Agassiz continued to study the evolution of fish while maintaining the medical career urged upon him by his parents. In October 1831, in what was to be a sadly ironic turn of events, he seized the opportunity to travel to Paris to study a grim cholera epidemic. He wasted no time in presenting himself to Cuvier. The great man was impressed with Agassiz's work and took a liking to the enthusiastic young Swiss, perhaps seeing reflections of his younger self in the bold-featured youth nervously spreading his research before him.

Cuvier turned over to Agassiz one of his elaborately equipped laboratories and all his personal notes on the subject of their mutual interest. The topic of fish fossils also held a fascination for Cuvier, and realizing that Agassiz had independently arrived at similiar conclusions, he was unceasingly generous in his aid, providing advice and encouragement whenever needed, even the occasional meal at his home where many contemporary original thinkers mingled over wine and cigars.

In May of 1832 tragedy struck. Cuvier was taken by the very cholera Agassiz had originally come to Paris to study. The impact of this painful event on Agassiz was profound:

> With Cuvier's death, whatever sense of intellectual independence Agassiz had known disappeared. The fact that the great naturalist had turned over important fossils to him for description and publication made Agassiz think of himself as Cuvier's disciple. He determined to model his intellectual efforts after the pattern set for him by Cuvier.[3]

Agassiz adopted Cuvier's conclusion that the earth's history had been periodically marked by great catastrophes that had destroyed existing plants and animals and wiped clean the slate for the creation of new creatures by God. These ideas, known as *catastrophism* and *special creation*, were concepts Agassiz would hold for the rest of his life and were fundamental to his physical view of the world.

The first, catastrophism, was a conclusion based upon the fossil record, an interpretation of the known facts. But the second idea, special creation, drifted from the precision of scientific data into the murky arena of theological dispute.

Agassiz's adoption of Cuvier's notion of special creation violates one of the basic principles of modern science: the concept of the invariance of physical laws. Scientists today assume that the physical laws governing our planet (for example, gravity) apply throughout the universe and are constant throughout time and space. Catastrophists assume that supernatural forces (God) can, and do, intervene in the affairs of our planet. Physical laws, in their view, are subject to the whims of supernatural forces. They also assume that the Bible is the ultimate authority as to the age of the earth. Many, even today, believe that the world was created in seven days and that it is only thousands of years old. The idea of special creation goes one step further: life is specially created after catastrophes occur.

Catastrophism (as it was understood by Agassiz and Cuvier) was the accepted geological assumption based upon the teachings of the Bible. It has now been rejected by the vast majority of scientists. The tradition that eventually overtook and replaced catastrophism was created by a Scottish amateur geologist, James Hutton (1726–97). He realized that over great periods of time, even small changes caused by the daily impact of forces such as wind and water would eventually transform the face of the earth. However, Hutton's motives in proposing a new approach to the earth sciences were not the strict scientific ones that we are now led to believe. He lived in a time before the notion of progress, so fundamental to our own era, was widely accepted. The Bible was still the ultimate authority on questions of the earth's history. The biblical account of the Great Flood was believed to be the key to understanding geology. Common thinking was that time brought only decay, not progress. It was generally assumed that the history of the planet could be divided into three phases:

> . . . firstly, there had been a period of generation extending from the Creation up to the Fall of Man; secondly, there was the prolonged and present period of degeneration

39

initiated by the Fall; and thirdly, there was the eagerly awaited period of regeneration that would be ushered in by Christ's Second Coming.[4]

Hutton challenged this view by arguing in the first volume of the *Transactions of the Royal Society of Edinburgh* (1788) that the earth's history was very long and would extend indefinitely into the future: ". . . we find no vestige of a beginning — no prospect of an end." He saw the earth as a vast machine created by the Almighty for the *purpose* of maintaining life (as opposed to the catastrophists, who were willing to believe that the Almighty could destroy life). His famous book, *Theory of the Earth with Proofs and Illustrations* (1795) was an attempt to show that the earth was the handiwork of God:

> If we believe that there is almighty power, and supreme wisdom employed for sustaining that beautiful system of plants and animals which is so interesting to us, we must certainly conclude, that the earth, on which this system of living things depends, has been constructed on principles that are adequate to the end proposed, and procure it a perfection which it is our business to explore.[5]

Hutton rejected the biblical idea of a deluge or great flood *because* he believed that this was contrary to God's design. If the purpose of the earth was to sustain life, then surely God would not violate His plan by allowing deluges to wreak havoc with His creation: "But, surely, general deluges form no part of the theory of the earth; for, the purpose of this earth is evidently to maintain vegetable and animal life, and not to destroy them."[6]

What was radical in Hutton's theory was his assumption that the earth's design was a more accurate reflection of the Almighty's intentions than was the Bible. And even more unusual was his belief that all geological phenomena could be understood as a product of a perfectly designed machine that was operating today as it has *always* operated. For Hutton, "the present was the key to the past." Given a vast amount of time, even small changes could result in significant results. Here we have Hutton writing as most geologists would like to remember him:

> Not only are no powers to be employed that are not natural to the globe, no action to be admitted of except those of which we know the principle, and no extraordinary events to be alleged in order to explain a common appearance, the powers of nature are not to be employed in order to destroy the very object of those powers; we are not to make nature act in violation to that order which we actually observe, and in subversion of created things. In whatever manner, therefore, we are to employ the great agents, fire and water, for producing those things which appear, it ought to be in such a way as is consistent with the propagation of plants and life of animals upon the surface of the earth. Chaos and confusion are not to be introduced into the order of nature, because certain things appear to our partial views as being in some disorder. Nor are we to proceed in feigning cause, when those seem insufficient which occur in our experience.[7]

Hutton wished to replace the chaos of the Great Flood with a world order more worthy of God. His idea of gradual change operating over vast amounts of time would come to be known as "uniformitarianism."

Charles Lyell (1797–1875), in *Principles of Geology* (1830 and 1832), took Hutton's idea of uniformitarianism, refined it, expanded it, and demonstrated it in language and with illustrations that were accessible to the nonscientist. He dealt a fatal blow to the notion that physical laws could be subject to the whims of supernatural forces. In opposition to catastrophism, he wrote:

> In our attempt to unravel these difficult questions, we shall adopt a different course, restricting ourselves to the known or possible operations of existing causes: feeling assured that we have not yet exhausted the resources which the study of the present course of nature may

provide, and therefore that we are not authorized, in the infancy of our science, to recur to extraordinary agents.[8]

In his time, and for more than a century, Lyell's prohibition against consideration of geological forces that cannot be observed in the present served the fledgling science of geology well. But Lyell was blind to the fact that these rigid boundaries need not exclude the investigation of extraordinary upheavals that can be explained without reference to a supernatural force — that is, dramatic geological upheavals (still subject to the physical laws of the earth) that result in accelerated rates of change.

These "spurts" of change occur as a result of physical events operating within the confines of natural laws.[9] Today, Cuvier's theory should be recognized as being far ahead of his time but geologists have grouped his ideas with the catastrophists' and his notion of a great geological upheaval was forgotten. His student, Louis Agassiz, took up the banner with his theory of the Ice Ages.

Four years after Cuvier's death, Agassiz was exploring Switzerland's sheer crevices and towering mountains with two friends, who were students of Alpine glaciers. The germ of an idea was planted as the two persuaded Agassiz that the dominating boulders they were climbing over had been pushed, heaved, and hauled to their positions by glaciers. Agassiz saw the possibilities at once and in 1837 he announced his theory of the Ice Ages to an unsuspecting Europe. "Siberian winter," he declared,

> . . . established itself for a time over a world previously covered with rich vegetation and peopled with large mammalia, similar to those now inhabiting the warm regions of India and Africa. Death enveloped all nature in a shroud, and the cold, having reached its highest degree, gave to this mass of ice at the maximum tension, the greatest possible hardness![10]

Although the term "Ice Ages" has become a part of our modern vocabulary, it was an unusual and startling concept when Agassiz first proposed it. Hand in hand with our concept of the Ice Ages comes the meaning of the term "glacial." Today it is generally accepted as indicating a ponderous slow movement, an inch-by-inch advancement (and thus losing its original sense of catastrophe). But Louis Agassiz, in first proposing that the earth had suffered traumatic periods of extreme cold, insisted that the Ice Ages had descended upon the earth suddenly and catastrophically, plunging it into its darkest winter:

> A sudden intense winter, that was to last for ages, fell upon our globe; it spread over the very countries where these tropical animals had their homes, and so suddenly did it come upon them that they were embalmed beneath masses of snow and ice, without time even for the decay which follows death.[11]

To Agassiz this theory of catastrophic Ice Ages cleared the overgrown trail leading to the heart of the mystery of extinctions. The onslaught of a sudden deadly Ice Age would have entombed massive creatures where they stood, mute witnesses to a season of disaster.

When Louis Agassiz first presented the idea of Ice Ages to the scientific community in 1837, he was met with great skepticism. However, Agassiz proved that the movement of glaciers could account for the placement of massive boulders. The skeptics were forced to accept that the earth had indeed once been gripped by deadly winters. The trigger for these paralyzing winters remained a puzzle. Agassiz had recognized this obstacle from the beginning:

> We have as yet no clew [sic] to the source of this great and sudden change of climate. Various suggestions have been made — among others, that formerly the inclination of the earth's axis was greater, or that a submersion of the continents under water might have produced a decided increase of cold; but none of these explanations are satisfactory, and science has yet to find any cause which accounts for all the phenomena connected with it.[12]

In 1842, the first clue (an unexpected astronomical one) was discovered by a mathematician working as a tutor in Paris. Joseph Alphonse Adhemar knew that the earth passes through four cardinal points (the spring equinox, the summer solstice, the fall equinox, and finally the winter solstice) during its orbit around the sun. One season changes to another as the earth crosses these points.

The cardinal points gradually shift over a grand, twenty-two-thousand-year cycle due to the gravitational pull of the sun, moon, and planets upon the earth. Adhemar knew that the earth is closest to the sun on January 3 and farthest away on July 4. At the present point in the orbit's grand cycle, those in the northern hemisphere are nearest to the warmth of the sun, resulting in relatively mild winters. But eventually, in thousands of years, around the time of the summer solstice, the earth will be drawn closer to the sun, precipitating sweltering summers and frigid winters. Adhemar believed that this gradual shifting of the cardinal points, which scientists today call the *precession of the equinoxes*, instigated the Ice Ages by depriving the earth of the sun's genial influence at critical times.

In 1843, another French scientist, Urbain Leverrier (1811–77), detected a second astronomical feature related to the Ice Ages. He realized that the distance that the earth travelled from the sun was affected by the actual *shape* of the earth's orbit. Over a one-hundred-thousand-year cycle, the orbit's shape is gradually altered, again by the gravitational influences of the sun, moon, and other planets. It ranges from a near perfect circle, as it is today, to a more oval orbit during which our world is carried farther from the sun, allowing the Ice Ages to gain a grip on the vulnerable earth.

Despite these breakthroughs in astronomy, there was still no agreement about the cause or timing of the Ice Ages. An unlikely source provided the third and final clue. Scotsman James Croll (1821–90) was forced to drop out of school at the age of thirteen to help his mother raise their family. But although his formal classes had ended, he undertook an ambitious self-education program during which he mastered the fundamentals of the physical sciences. In 1859, after holding numerous jobs, from millwright to insurance salesman, he finally arrived at the position from which he made his monumental contribution to science: Croll became the janitor in the Andersonian College and Museum in Glasgow. He wrote: "My salary was small, it is true, little more than sufficient to enable me to subsist; but this was compensated by advantages for me of another kind."[13] The janitor had access to the college's science library. It was all he needed.

The untutored Croll decided to turn his talents to the puzzle that still eluded the scientific establishment — what had actually caused the Ice Ages? With the publication of his book *Climate and Time* (1872), Croll introduced the third astronomical key to the mystery — movement of the earth's axis or tilt.

The angle of the earth's tilt determines the amount of sunshine received by various parts of the planet. Changes in the tilt result in temperature changes on the earth's surface. Today the axis is angled at 23.4 degrees. But the tilt gradually changes, varying from a minimum of 21.8 degrees to a maximum of 24.4 degrees.

Milutin Milankovitch (1857–1927), a Serbian engineer, who in 1911 was working as a professor of mathematics at the University of Belgrade, used these astronomical factors to calculate the amount of solar radiation that would reach the earth at any particular time in its history. He believed that Ice Ages resulted when winter ice did not melt the following summer because the earth was not receiving enough warmth from the sun. Over successive seasons the ice sheets would thicken, slowly smothering the land beneath.

In 1976, Croll's and Milankovitch's ideas were validated by James Hay, John Imbrie, and Nicholas Shackleton, who published a paper[14] showing that the geological evidence of the Ice Ages matched the astronomical cycles. They showed that normally the earth is wrapped in a *Glacial Epoch*, and that we now enjoy a very mild climate compared to what the planet normally endures.

The present inter-glacial reign, which began almost twelve thousand years ago, is destined to be only a short-lived melting period. During the last 350,000 years, there have been four inter-glacial periods occurring roughly 335,000, 220,000, 127,000, and 11,600 years ago. Three astronomical cycles must coincide to bring about an inter-glacial period: the planet's tilt must reach approximately 24.4 degrees; the orbit's shape must be elongated by at least 1 percent; and finally, the earth must be closest to the sun in the month of June.

The Croll/Milankovitch astronomical theory of the Ice Ages is today gathering widespread support as an explanation for the *timing* of large-scale glacial epochs. But it addresses only part of the question. Of equal importance is the *geography* of glaciation. It is here that the long-neglected theory of earth crust displacement plays its role in unravelling the mystery. According to Hapgood's theory, the areas of the globe that experience the coldest climates are those that are thrust into the polar zones.

In his foreword to Hapgood's book, Albert Einstein explains the mechanism that might dislocate the crust:

> In a polar region there is continual disposition of ice, which is not symmetrically distributed about the pole. The earth's rotation acts on these unsymmetrically deposited masses, and produces centrifugal momentum that is transmitted to the rigid crust of the earth. The constantly increasing centrifugal momentum produced this way will, when it reaches a certain point, produce a movement of the earth's crust over the rest of the earth's body, and this will displace the polar regions toward the equator.[15]

And it will, simultaneously, shift some temperate areas into the polar regions, freezing them until they are freed by another earth crust displacement.

Einstein, although convinced that displacements had occurred, doubted that the weight of the ice caps alone would be of sufficient force to dislodge the crust. Hapgood gave up searching for the cause of the displacements and concentrated on demonstrating how his theory could explain unsolved problems in geology and evolution.

The Croll/Milankovitch theory of Ice Ages suggests a combined extraterrestrial gravitational pull of the planets, sun, and moon and the terrestrial influence of the weight of the ice caps as a cause for the crustal displacements. We suggest that if the shape of the earth's orbit deviates from a perfect circle by more than 1 percent, the gravitational influence of the sun increases because its path is narrower at points. The sun exercises more pull upon the planet and its massive ice sheets. Their ponderous weight alternately pushes and pulls against the crust and this immense pressure, combined with the greater incline in the earth's tilt and the sun's increased gravitational pull, forces the crust to shift.

After each displacement the ice sheets melt, raising the ocean level. This melting is compounded if the displacement coincides with the beginning of an interglacial period when worldwide temperatures climb. Such was the case 11,600 years ago following the last earth crust displacement. Eventually, as snowfall again accumulates within the Arctic and Antarctic circles, the ocean returns to a lower level and the cycle begins all over.

The last earth crust displacement occurred 11,600 years ago when all three astronomical cycles meshed, ushering in the present interglacial epoch. The dominant cycle in these events is that of the earth's tilt (now thought to move from the minimum of 21.8 degrees to 24.4 degrees every 41,000 years). We believe other earth crust displacements occurred during the last glacial epochs at 52,600 and 93,600 years ago. Such a theory, coupled with Hapgood's geomagnetic evidence for the location of the "poles," accounts for the unique geography of glaciation. Those areas trapped within the polar zones both before and after the displacements accumulate unusually great amounts of glaciation.

This grand cycle of destruction may, as Cuvier guessed, have been the cause of periodic bouts of mass extinctions. There have been many of these disasters, each one of which has had a profound impact upon the course of evolution. The "late Pleistocene Extinctions," which occurred shortly after 9600 B.C., have been studied in detail by scientists attempting to solve the mystery of these deadly events.

Another line of inquiry puts the blame upon humankind.

Charles Darwin's co-discoverer of the theory of natural selection, Alfred Russel Wallace (1823–1913), advanced the idea that the extinctions at the end of the last Ice Age were caused not only by climatic changes, but also by humans. In 1911 he wrote:

> ... the extinction of so many large Mammalia is actually due to man's agency, *acting in co-operation with those general causes* which at the culmination of each geological era has led to the extinction of the larger, the most specialised, or the most strangely modified forms ... (italics in original)[16]

Like Darwin, he was strongly committed to the Hutton/Lyell model of strict gradual change in the earth's history. But even Lyell couldn't ignore the problems in resting all the terrible responsibility for extinctions upon humans:

> It is probable that causes more general and powerful than the agency of Man, alterations in climate, variations in the range of many species of animals, vertebrate and inverte-brate, and of plants, geographical changes in the height, depth, and extent of land and sea, or all of these com-bined, have given rise, in a vast series of years, to the annihilation . . . of many large mammals.[17]

Despite Lyell's warnings, the idea of humankind as the cause of extinctions has a great following among anthropologists and pale-ontologists. The modern spokesman for "the overkill hypothesis" is Dr. Paul S. Martin of the University of Arizona. He believes that human migration to the New World caused the mass extinctions. And North America certainly did experience massive extinctions at this time. The massive bears, sabre-toothed lions, mammoths, and mastodons all became extinct shortly after 9600 B.C. Many archae-ologists believe that people first arrived in the New World shortly after 9600 B.C., an idea we will examine in detail later. Martin conjectures that the animals that humans encountered had not developed the necessary skills to escape the newcomers' hunting techniques and were consequently slaughtered to extinction.[18] In contrast, the animals of the Old World, especially Europe and Africa, had evolved evasive strategies to deal with hunters, thereby avoid-ing the fate of their counterparts in the New World.

It is perhaps a natural view to adopt in the late twentieth century, given our shameful record in annihilating so many species, but the overkill hypothesis can only explain one set of mass extinctions, it can't explain mass extinctions that occurred earlier than the Pleistocene. Nor can the overkill theory explain the deaths of vast numbers of large animals that once thrived in a temperate northern Siberia, land that is now barren tundra. To support these animals Siberia's climate must have been much warmer than it is today.

Russian scientists are convinced that humankind played little or no role in their extinction and that only a dramatic climatic change can account for so many deaths.[19]

The physical facts are not in dispute. Various continents have experienced different rates of extinction at different times. Nearly twelve thousand years ago, North America, South America, Australia, and the Arctic regions suffered massive extinctions while, at the same time, there were relatively few in Europe and Africa.[20] These varying rates of disappearance would seem, at first glance, to support the overkill hypothesis:

> The lack of synchroneity between the extinctions on different continents and their variable intensity, for example, heavier in America than Africa, appears to eliminate as a cause any sudden extraterrestrial or cosmic catastrophe.[21]

But an earth crust displacement would cause extinctions to occur on different continents at different rates as a result of varying changes in the world's latitudes. Some continents experience great climatic change while others are largely unaffected. Changing climates produce extinctions as creatures succumb to different temperatures and alien seasons.

Hapgood's data permit us to see the Pleistocene extinctions in a clear light. Using his determination of the location of the earth's crust before 9600 B.C., we can observe the latitude changes that occurred after the displacement. An imaginary circle drawn around the globe, through the locations of the North and South poles, reveals the area that suffered the greatest trauma. We call it the *line of greatest displacement* (LGD). This line runs through North America, west of South America, bisects Antarctica, travels through Southeast Asia, goes on to Siberia, and then back to North America. The ring corresponds directly with those regions of the globe that suffered the most extinctions.[22]

The *line of least displacement* (LLD) intersects with those climatic regions that remained relatively stable both during and after the catastrophe. It runs through Greenland, Europe, and Africa before cutting between Australia and New Zealand, passing Hawaii, and then returning to Greenland. This LLD corresponds directly with those regions that experienced the least extinctions.[23] (See Maps 6a and 6b.)

Unlike the overkill hypothesis, the theory of earth crust displacement provides a model for the study of mass extinctions in general. The same principle can be applied to earlier geological periods and is not dependent upon our guesses as to the ability of animals to avoid human hunters. An earth crust displacement randomly determines which species will survive and which will perish. The remnants of species that survive the destruction of an earth crust displacement represent smaller gene pools increasing the probability of the development of new species because mutations can take a better "hold" within small communities. Ocean creatures stand a much greater chance because they can swim to climates to which they are already adapted. Land animals, however, have their

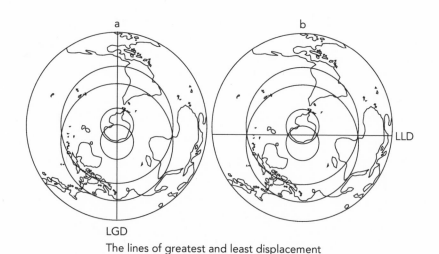

The lines of greatest and least displacement

Maps 6a & 6b: Each earth crust displacement results in dramatic climatic changes. Some regions experience far more drastic latitude change than others. The last displacement left a path of extinction across the line of greatest shift. Along the line of least displacement extinctions were few. North America lost large mammals such as mammoths and sabre-toothed tigers, while Africa's elephants and lions survived.

mobility hampered by mountains, deserts, lakes, and oceans. With escape cut off, they must adapt, or extinction is inevitable. This explains why evolution appears to occur faster on land than within the oceans.

The most recent earth crust displacement left its evidence in a ring of death around the globe. All the continents along the line of greatest displacement experienced mass extinctions while the continents closest to the line of least displacement experienced relatively few. The mass graves of so many giant creatures bear last witness to the great upheavals that periodically shatter our planet.

Human beings shared the fate of many other species. Myths are told of a lost island paradise that was ripped apart, drowned, and finally suffocated within a shroud of snow.

Chapter Five The Lost Island Paradise

Off the northwest coast of Canada lie 150 islands known as the Queen Charlottes. This fog-swept, rugged area cradles some of the oldest living forests in the New World and is home to a remarkable tribe, the Haida. The Haida had elaborate traditions and rituals, dispersing their wealth in a ceremony known as the "potlach." Accomplished boat builders and great hunters, they paddled huge cedar canoes along the Pacific coast in search of salmon, seal, and even whale.

The Haida's wood, shell, and bone carvings are world-famous. But their art reaches its fullest expression in the haunting features of the totem poles that still stand guard in some isolated inlets.

Like the Egyptians and Greeks, the Haida feared for the safety of their home when earthquakes shook the land. But they placed their faith in a god who restrained the buckling of the earth and secured the sky from falling:

> . . . Sacred-One-Standing-and-Moving . . . is the Earth-Supporter; he himself rests upon a copper box, which . . . is conceived as a boat; from his breast rises the Pillar of the Heavens, extending to the sky; his movements are the cause of earthquakes.[1]

If the Earth-Supporter ever lost control of the Pillar of the Heavens, the ensuing catastrophic effects would mirror the events of an earth crust displacement: earthquakes, a falling sky, and a worldwide flood.

Over generations, many stories are told around the world which, like the Haida myth, weave a narrative that can explain the horrifying memory of a falling sky.

Some archaeologists date the Haida's arrival in the Queen Charlotte Islands to almost twelve thousand years ago.[2] The Haida believed that before the Great Flood their ancestors lived in a magnificent city in a distant land:

> . . . the great chief of the heavens . . . decided to punish this great village . . . he caused the river waters to rise. Soon the rivers and creeks all over the country began to swell. Some of the people escaped to hills, while others embarked in their large canoes. Still the waters were rising higher and higher until only the high mountain peaks showed above the swollen water . . . [the Haida ancestors landed on a mountain top] . . . When the Flood was over, the lost stone anchors were found there, at the place where they had anchored their canoes.[3]

The Haida's dialect is the oldest branch of the "Na-Dene" family of American native languages.[4] Na-Dene, according to recent Russian investigations,[5] is related to the language of the Sumerians who created the world's first known civilization in what is now known as Iraq six thousand years ago.

In northern Syria, on a mound overlooking the Euphrates River, archaeologists have discovered one of the oldest remains of agriculture in the world.[6] For hundreds of thousands of years, people in this part of the world lived by hunting and gathering. Suddenly within the same century as the fall of Atlantis, they turned to agriculture. Radiocarbon dating at a site called "Tell Abu Hureya," showed that by 9500 B.C., some early villagers had begun to practise farming alongside their hunting and gathering, domesticating wild rabbits, goats, and sheep, and wild wheat, rye, and barley. From these early developments arose what archaeologists believe was the first civilization after Atlantis — Sumeria — which began to flourish around 3300 B.C.

Three gods were of particular importance to the Sumerians. The first, "Enlil," was known as the "Lord of the Air" and the king of kings. He was the most worshipped and feared god for he had within his power the most destructive weapon: the power of the flood. "The word of Enlil is a breath of wind, the eye sees it not. His word is a deluge which advances and has no rival."[7]

The second great god was "Enki," who was the "Lord of the Earth" and the god of waters. As the story is told, the Sumerians believed Enki to have been their saviour at the time of the flood. Enki overhears a conspiracy between the flood-god Enlil and the third great god, the sky-god "An," in which they plan to destroy mankind with their combined powers. Enki decides to save one man and his family from the coming disaster. He chooses Ziusudra, who is a king and priest living on the island of Dilmun. A later Babylonian myth records the words of Enki: "Destroy thy house, build a vessel, Leave thy riches, seek thy life, Store in thy vessel the seeds of all life."[8]

In the original Sumerian tale we learn the fate of Ziusudra's ark:

When for seven days and seven nights,
The Flood had raged over the land,
And the huge boat had been tossed on the great water by
the storms,
The Sun-god arose shedding light in Heaven and on Earth.
Ziusudra made an opening in the side of the great ship.
He let the light of the hero Sun-god enter into the great
ship.
Ziusudra, the king,
Before the Sun-god he bowed his face to the ground.[9]

Ziusudra's ark comes to rest on the top of a mountain somewhere in the Middle East. Like Noah, he and his family must begin life anew.

In 1899–1900, a team of American archaeologists unearthed thirty-five thousand tablets, the written records of this civilization, from the ancient Sumerian city of Nippur, a city dedicated to the flood-god, Enlil. The archaeologists were understandably excited — such a find could reveal the very roots of civilization. And according to the tablets, those roots were to be found in Dilmun, a mountainous island in the ocean. Most of its people were said to have perished when the sky-god conspired with Enlil to destroy humankind. The survivors escaped the flood in a great ship, in which they stored "the seeds of all life," to a mountain near Nippur.[10] The island paradise from which they had fled lay across the Indian Ocean[11] towards the *south*: towards Antarctica.

The rain-drenched forests of the Queen Charlottes lie half a world away from the sun-baked plains of Iraq, yet the Haida and the Sumerians share a remarkably similar story of their origins:

HAIDA MYTH	SUMERIAN MYTH
Long ago, our ancestors lived in the world's largest village. Life was care-free until the great chief of the heavens decided to destroy mankind by changing the sky and bringing a worldwide flood.	Long ago, our ancestors lived on the island of Dilmun. Life was care-free until the sky-god and flood-god decided to destroy mankind by changing the sky and bringing a worldwide flood.
Survivors escaped in large canoes which took them to a new land where they landed on a mountain.	Survivors escaped in a large ship which took them to a new land where they landed on a mountain.
A new era began.	A new era began.

It is unlikely that the ancient Sumerians could have made contact with the peoples of the Pacific coast of America, yet their mythology and language share critical elements. Could it be that they also share a common heritage — a common lost paradise?

•

Anyone who attempts the 4,350-metre climb up the rough winding road to Lake Titicaca in the Peruvian Andes gasps as the thin mountain air evades their lungs. But the struggle is worth it, for at the summit lies a mysterious lake. Only the graceful reed boats of the native people who still fish its depths and the restless winds of the past disturb the calm surface of this, the highest major lake in the world. The Inca claim that their ancestors came here in the remote past to construct the great city of Tiahuanaco with its massive Temple of the Sun. The city was built from massive boulders, comparable to those of the Egyptian pyramids. But the construction is incomplete, as if it had been abruptly abandoned. A Polish researcher, Arthur Posnansky (1874–1946), spent the better part of his life trying to unravel the mystery of Tiahuanaco.

No one has spent more time or effort studying Tiahuanaco's ruins on Lake Titicaca than Posnansky, and he concluded that the Temple of the Sun had been constructed more than ten thousand years ago, almost at the same time as we believe Atlantis was destroyed. Posnansky was convinced of the reality of the Great Flood, and in one amazing passage he offers a prophetic conclusion:

> The face of the earth has with the passage of time undergone great transformations. Where today we find the arctic region covered with a vast tunic of ice, there lies hidden, perhaps, in an impenetrable silence, the ground which in very remote epochs was the dwelling place of great concentrated masses of human beings.[12]

The same words could apply to the Antarctic region.

In the centre of Tiahuanaco, the massive Temple of the Sun is aligned with the rising sun, as are the pyramids of Egypt and Mexico. However, there is a slight discrepancy in its angles. Posnansky reasoned that if the ancient builders were capable of constructing massive monuments in the thin air of the high Andes, then surely they could accurately align their holy temple with the rising sun on the summer solstice. It occurred to him that perhaps the boulders were correctly aligned when first erected but gradual alterations of the earth's axis over a long period of time had resulted in what now, at first glance, appeared to be a misalignment. If the temple had been properly aligned when it was first built then a date could be estimated based upon the precession of the equinoxes. Posnansky concluded that the temple was correctly aligned to a date ". . . somewhere beyond ten thousand years."[13]

Archaeologists have dismissed this notion as fantasy. It is simply not possible, in their view, for a civilization to have existed at such an early date. This would be four thousand years older than Sumeria (the "first" civilization of world archaeology). Posnansky's research has consequently been ignored and his calculations have never been tested by other researchers.

However, Posnansky's estimated date for the construction of the Temple of the Sun on Lake Titicaca has recently been given a boost with the unexpected discovery of the age of the Great Sphinx of ancient Egypt. Two methods have been used to date the construction of the Sphinx: one using evidence of erosion and the other using the same precessional method employed by Posnansky.

The idea that the Sphinx might be much older than Egyptian civilization was first proposed in the late 1940s by the French scholar, R.A. Schwaller de Lubicz. In *Le roi de la theocratie pharaonique* (*Sacred Science* in the English version), Schwaller claimed that the Great Sphinx had experienced extensive *water* erosion. We all know that the Sphinx lies in a vast desert where rain is an uncommon phenomenon. In 1972, John Anthony West focused on this insight of Schwaller and included it in his book, *Serpent in the Sky: The High Wisdom of Ancient Egypt*.[14] The revolutionary idea that the Sphinx might predate Egyptian civilization was too radical an idea for Eygptologists to consider. They ignored it, preferring silence to debate.

West continued to explore the idea into the late 1980s. Eventually, he interested a respected geologist from the University of Boston, Dr. Robert M. Schoch, in his work. Schoch was skeptical but curious. He went to Egypt with West to see for himself the weathering patterns on the Sphinx.

It soon became clear to Schoch that the Sphinx had indeed been weathered by rain for thousands of years before the desert claimed the region. Wind erosion cuts sharp, straight patterns into sediment layers. But the Sphinx exhibits the rounded, furrowed contours typical of water erosion. This meant that the monument must have been constructed during a long rainy period sometime before 5000 B.C. and very possibly much earlier. Since this pre-dates the appearance of Egyptian civilization by thousands of years, the question was at once raised: who carved the Great Sphinx?

On October 23, 1991, Schoch presented his conclusions to the Geological Society of America. His data were accepted at once.

Schoch and West had begun to turn back the clock of human history by thousands of years. They next took their argument to Chicago in 1992 before the American Association for the Advancement of Science. Once again support was forthcoming from geologists, but Egyptologists simply could not accept such an ancient age for the Sphinx. It *must* be incorrect, so their reasoning went, for the alternative was to suggest a notion that, as one Egyptologist claimed, undermined "everything we know about ancient Egypt."[15]

In the fall of 1993, and again in the summer of 1994, West presented his documentary, *The Mystery of the Sphinx*, on U.S. television. The arguments were now too strong to be ignored. It was clear that the very existence of the Sphinx and the impressive temples standing in front of it, built with stones weighing more than 180 metric tons, was evidence for the existence of a long-lost ancient, yet advanced, civilization.

In 1994, another remarkable event occurred with the publication of Robert Bauval and Adrian Gilbert's *The Orion Mystery*.[16] They discovered that the layout of Egypt's great pyramids followed the pattern of the constellation Orion as it would have appeared in the year 10,450 B.C. Orion, representing a giant star-belted god striding across the heavens, appears near the Milky Way, which to the Egyptians seemed to flow in an immense stream across the heavens. Its counterpart on earth was the Nile River. The three pyramids of Giza mirror the positions of the three stars of Orion's "belt."

Bauval and Gilbert, using precessional astronomy, dated the actual construction of the Great Pyramid to 2450 B.C. But unexpectedly, they discovered that although the massive stones were placed at this time, the layout of the pyramids depicted the pattern of Orion at the much earlier time of 10,450 B.C. Bauval and Gilbert concluded that this date corresponded to what the ancient Egyptians called the "First Time." The "First Time" in Egyptian mythology was an age when the gods entrusted mortals, the first pharaohs, with the laws and wisdom that would enable them to rule Egypt.

The Great Sphinx, as part of the Giza pyramid complex, is also orientated to the "First Time" (10,450 B.C.) and may actually have been built then. It would seem entirely possible that the Great

Sphinx is a remnant of a much larger project constructed sometime after 10,450 B.C. The discoveries of Bauval and Gilbert, when coupled with the research of West and Schoch, hint at the possibility that there are much older structures, physically connected to the Great Sphinx, hidden beneath the pyramids.

Now two sciences, geology and astronomy, were pushing back humankind's achievements to a time well before any known civilization. Bauval and Gilbert's astronomical evidence follows the same assumptions used in dating the Temple of the Sun on Lake Titicaca, measurements that had led Posnansky to conclude that an advanced civilization once existed. But what of these incredible architects of the Sphinx and Temple of the Sun? How and why did they perish?

The tale is told by the Aymara, who still live on the shores of Lake Titicaca. The Aymara are a very ancient and proud race. More than two and a half million people speak the Aymara language, raise llamas, and grow potatoes on the lake's shore — just as their ancestors have for thousands of years. Even the renowned Inca Empire borrowed heavily from their ancient customs of sun worship, agriculture, and the use of llamas.[17]

The Aymara tell of strange events at Titicaca after the Great Flood. Strangers attempted to build a great city on the lake. An Aymara myth retold by an early Spanish visitor tells of how their ancestors crossed over Lake Titicaca and with their warriors ". . . waged such a war on the people of which I speak that he killed them all."[18]

After struggling so long and so hard to survive the ravages brought by the last earth crust displacement, these people perished, not at the hands of nature, but by the spears and arrows of their own species. Something drove the Aymara to rise in rebellion against the foreigners. Perhaps the Aymara were forced to labour on the great city of Tiahuanaco? Did they discover that the strangers were not, after all, gods? Were the Aymara outraged by the prospect of labouring for mere mortals?

The Aymara's contribution is not confined to a distant myth whispered by the waves lapping among the reeds of Lake Titicaca. When the computer (the twentieth century's unique wand) passes over the Aymara language, it reveals an amazing secret.

In 1984, Ivan Guzman de Rojas, a Bolivian mathematician, scored a notable first in the development of computer software by showing that Aymara could be used as an intermediate language for simultaneously translating English into several other languages. Guzman's "Atamiri" (the Aymara word for interpreter) was used as a translator by the Panama Canal Commission in a commercial test with Wang Laboratories. How did Guzman accomplish a task using a simple personal computer that experts at eleven European universities, using advanced computers, failed to complete?

> . . . his system's secret, which solved a problem that had stumped machine translation experts around the world, is the rigid, logical and unambiguous structure of Aymara, ideal for transformation into a computer algorithm.[19]

> Aymara is rigorous and simple — which means that its syntactical rules always apply, and can be written out concisely in the sort of algebraic shorthand that computers understand. Indeed, such is its purity that some historians think it did not just evolve, like other languages, but was actually constructed from scratch . . .[20]

The Aymara were productive farmers, but is it likely that they would spend their leisure time constructing a language? Such a development is more likely the product of an advanced civilization, one capable of constructing the Temple of the Sun and the Great Sphinx. Could it have been the survivors of the lost island paradise who gave the Aymara a language so precise, so grammatically pure, that it would become a tool for the most advanced technology of our own century? What other advances in science might we glean from a language spoken by peasants on the highlands near Lake Titicaca?

After studying the mythology of the Aymara and raking over the remains of their Temple of the Sun, Arthur Posnansky concluded that Tiahuanaco, the abandoned city on Lake Titicaca, was originally populated by the people from "Aztlan," the lost island paradise of the Aztecs.[21]

The Aztecs ruled a vast empire that stretched the length and width of Central America. In the spring of 1519, they became terrified that their world was coming to an end.

•

Imagine the following scene: it is almost sunset.[22] Montezuma, priest, warrior, astronomer, and first Lord of the Aztecs, methodically prepares for his evening salutation to the sun. For these few moments the tumultuous empire of the Aztecs is at peace. Darkness approaches quickly as the sun slants behind the mountains that crowd Teotihuacan, Mexico. Montezuma drapes himself in the comfort of ancient rituals as he prepares to meet the night.

Two humble fishermen are brought into the hall to be presented to their venerated leader. The shuffle of their feet disturbs the temple's silence as they move towards him, avoiding his gaze and looking instead to the creature they drag behind them.

Montezuma's eyes dart towards the awkward bundle they so nervously offer him. It is a large grey crane, his ashy wings pinned against the fishermen's mesh net. Montezuma recognizes this important Aztec symbol. It is traditional on the tense morning of a battle that two feathers from the long-legged crane be inserted in each warrior's hair as a symbol of readiness to fight to the death. A strange, smoky mirror protrudes from the bird's head. The fishermen quiver, prepared for the worst if Montezuma is angered by his interpretation of this sign.

A smile touches his lips and the Lord of the Aztecs leans back, gathering his ceremonial robes around him. He dismisses the fishermen, showering them with compliments and treasures to reward their capture of this wonderful bird. Montezuma hopes that this unexpected omen means that Blue Hummingbird, god of war, has been transformed into a crane. Aztec legend dictates that the day Hummingbird is transformed into a sacred crane the Aztecs will conquer all their enemies.

As the last hot dust of the Mexican day sifts through the apertures in the temple's carved stone, Montezuma's shiver of anticipation is suddenly laced with fear.

As he watched the magical obsidian mirror, the scene changed to daytime over the sea and a sandy beach. Up from the waters came the strange bearded men on their hornless deer. They advanced and before them came fire and destruction.[23]

Montezuma gazes upon a vision of the destruction of his world.

The fear gnaws at him as he remembers other vile omens that have haunted the empire in recent years. In 1509, a great light appeared on the eastern horizon.[24] Later, three comets[25] and three terrifying earthquakes brought chaos to the Aztecs. Nature's furies were followed by a strange vision visited upon Montezuma's sister. She saw their precious capital destroyed by bearded men of grey stone who came from the sea.[26] Perhaps most ominous of all, for no apparent reason, the great lake upon which the Aztec capital rested began to flood.

Montezuma has not forgotten that in 1508, the year before the great light appeared on the eastern ocean, the planet of Venus, symbol of Quetzalcoatl, the Plumed Serpent, challenged the sun by crossing its path. Could this sign mean that Blue Hummingbird's hated enemy would be returning? Quetzalcoatl was the ancestral king and great god of the ancient Toltecs, former glorious rulers of Mexico before the Aztecs. Montezuma's personal bloodline is traceable to the imperious Toltecs. He is torn by the implication of the omens. How can he welcome the enemy of Blue Hummingbird?

His fear of disaster is tempered with his knowledge of the Plumed Serpent's reputation as a great god. It is Montezuma's duty to correctly interpret and act upon the omens. Everything depends upon it. No battle, however fierce, has ever disturbed his soul like the whisper of doubt that this twilight has brought. And now this crane, carrying a strange dull mirror reflecting disaster, has been placed at his feet. The people of the Aztec empire are restless and nervous. Wild rumours are everywhere — of floating mountains carrying odd strangers.

Montezuma is painfully aware that historical parallels are lining up against him. Ninth ruler of the Aztecs, he stands at the peak of their power and should be exulting in this honoured position. Instead he is torn by doubts and fears. The Toltecs also had nine kings before the Plumed Serpent left them and they fell from power.

Is he to be the ninth and final king of the Aztecs? The gods must be consulted.

He turns to the skies and the stars. From his astrological calculations and recollections of ancient myths, Montezuma calculates that the Plumed Serpent will return in One Reed Year.[27] One Reed Year occurs every fifty-two years — the next is due in 1519.

Montezuma waits, checking and rechecking his calculations. He now believes that he has narrowed the date of the Plumed Serpent's return to the very day. Surely, he reasons, the god will come back to his homeland on his name day, Nine Wind Day. On the European calendar it reads April 21, 1519. Montezuma sends spies to the eastern shores to watch for the coming of the god on this sacred day.

•

On April 21, 1519, the silence of Mexico's Caribbean coast was broken by the clang of swords and the shuffle of marching boots across the white beach. From his ship stepped a bearded conquistador named Hernando Cortes, his helmet adorned with "a plume of feathers."[28] The Spaniard pounded a great cross into the soft sand to honour his faith, little realizing that the cross was also the symbol of the Plumed Serpent.[29]

The Aztec spies watched in amazement and horror before hurrying back to Montezuma to confirm his prediction. Never in the course of human history has there been a greater case of mistaken identity. On that day, Cortes, with blind luck on his side, began a bloody march that would ultimately end in the annihilation of the Aztec empire.

The Spanish conquerors believed that Mexico was once an Egyptian colony. It is little wonder, since the Aztecs shared several common mythological themes with the Egyptians. The Egyptians believed that the world was surrounded on all sides, including the heavens, with water. In Aztec mythology:

> The sea was thought to extend outward and upward until — like the walls of a cosmic house — it merged with the sky . . . The sky, therefore, was known to contain waters

which might in perilous times descend in deluges, annihilating man.[30]

This empire, like that of the Egyptians, had built great pyramids
that symbolized the land that saved their ancestors from the flood.[31]
And like those of Egypt the solar megaliths were aligned with the
rising sun. It was atop the Temple of the Sun that Cortes met
Montezuma. He recounted their conversation in a letter to the King
of Spain. Montezuma told Cortes about the island homeland of the
Aztecs' ancestors: "Our fathers dwelt in that happy and prosperous
place which they called Aztlan, which means whiteness."[32]

Aztlan is described as ". . . a bright land of shining light and
whiteness which contained seven cities surrounding a sacred mountain."[33] Perhaps the blazing lights of Aztlan were actually the southern lights of Antarctica before that land was thrust into the confines
of the Antarctic Circle.

Aztlan was said to be ". . . located beyond the waters, or as
surrounded by waters; and the first stage of the migration is said to
have been made by boat."[34] Once again we have the familiar story:

> They believed that two persons survived the deluge, a
> man, named Coxcox, and his wife. Their heads are repre-
> sented in ancient paintings, together with a boat floating
> on the waters, at the foot of a mountain.[35]

Cortes's secretary and biographer, Francisco Lopez de Gomara,
also recorded information about Aztlan. His book, *Historia general da
las Indies* (1552), related that the original homeland of the Aztecs was
"Aztlan," a white island in the ocean. Gomara equated Aztlan with
Atlantis, based upon Plato's account. And in 1572, the historian
Pedro Sarmiento came to the same conclusion based upon south
American mythology. For three decades Atlantis was widely be-
lieved to be the original homeland of the native people of America.[36]

Throughout America the myth of a lost island paradise haunts
the memories of the native people. But they were not alone in their
grief for the lost land. Across the ocean the tale was told in India,
Iran, Iraq, and Japan.

•

In 1922, Mahatma Gandhi, about to be sentenced to six years in prison, said to the judge:

> "Since you have done me the honor of recalling the trial of the late Lokamaya Gangadhar Tilak, I just want to say that I consider it the proudest privilege and honor to be associated with his name.[37]

Bal Gangadhar Tilak forged the tactic of passive resistance as a means of overthrowing British rule in India. He was held in such esteem that Gandhi used the title "Lokamaya" ("Beloved Leader of the People") when referring to him. Tilak earned his title while imprisoned in 1897 for seditious writings; the British hoped to curb his role in the rising tide of Indian nationalism. The harsh conditions of his Bombay cell took their toll. Tilak's health waned. Fearing that his death in custody might spark a general uprising, the British moved the "Beloved Leader of the People" to a safer prison in Poona. Helped by donations of fruit and vegetables from his followers Tilak partially recovered his health. But soon a new hunger overtook him — the need for intellectual stimulation. Relief came from an unlikely quarter: England.

Tilak had published a respected work on India's oldest texts, the Vedas, and Sanskrit scholars at Oxford and Cambridge were outraged by his imprisonment and treatment. Professor F. Max Muller, the world's leading authority on the Vedas, was successful in having Tilak's case reviewed by Queen Victoria. She shortened his sentence and granted him a reading light in his cell. Denied access to newspapers or any other current material, Tilak used this "privilege" to continue his studies of the Vedas.

Upon his release Tilak retired to the mountains to rest at a favourite family retreat. In 1903 his great work, *The Arctic Home in the Vedas*, was published. In it he argued that the remains of an island paradise could be found beneath the Arctic Ocean: "It was the advent of the Ice Age that destroyed the mild climate of the original home and covered it into an ice-bound land unfit for the habitation of man."[38]

Tilak summarized a key passage in the oldest saga of Iran, the *Zend-Avesta*:

> Ahura Mazda warns Yima, the first king of men, of the approach of *a dire winter*, which is to destroy every living creature by *covering the land with a thick sheet of ice*, and advises Yima to build a Vara, or an enclosure, to preserve the seeds of every kind of animal and plant. The meeting is said to have taken place in the Airyana Vaêjo, or Paradise of the Iranians. (italics added)[39]

Tilak chose the Arctic Circle as the location of the lost continent of Airyana Vaêjo after reading *Paradise Found: The Cradle of the Human Race at the North Pole* (1885), written by the founder of Boston University, Dr. William Fairfield Warren. Warren had been impressed by how often the story of a falling sky and great flood was to be found intertwined with accounts of a lost island paradise. He also realized that the lost land had many polar features. In Warren's view, the worldwide nature of these descriptions suggested a common physical explanation. The exciting idea of Ice Ages provided part of his answer:

> Now if, during the prevalence of the Deluge, or later, in consequence of the on-coming of the Ice Age, the survivors of the Flood were translocated from their antediluvian home at the Pole to the great Central Asian "plateau of Pamir," the probable starting-point of historic postdiluvian humanity, the new aspect presented by the heavens in this new latitude would have been precisely as if in the grand world-convulsion the sky itself had become displaced, its polar dome tilted over about one third of the distance from the zenith to the horizon. The astronomical knowledge of those survivors very likely enabled them to understand the true reason of the changed appearance, but their rude descendants, unfavored with the treasures of antediluvian science, and born only to a savage or nomadic life in their new and inhospitable home, might easily have forgotten the explanation. In time such

children's children might easily have come to embody the strange story handed down from their fathers in strange myths, in which nothing of the original facts remained beyond an obscure account of some mysterious displacement of the sky, supposed to have occurred in a far-off age in connection with some appalling natural catastrophe or world-disaster.[40]

Warren conjectured that the island paradise myths and their dramatic accounts of a falling sky and worldwide flood were part of the actual history of traumatized populations who had lost their homeland in a geological upheaval. Again and again in the most ancient records Warren found evidence that the lost land was near the pole.

For example, in 681 A.D., the Japanese Emperor Temnu ordered the man with the greatest memory in the country, Hieda no Are, to recite the most ancient of myths to a scribe. Hieda no Are was the most respected voice of the "guild of narrators" (katari-be) and he took his task seriously. O no Yasumaro, the scribe, faithfully transcribed Hieda no Are's words. Their compilation became known as the Ko-ji-ki ("Records of Ancient Matters") and appeared in 712. Warren believed that the earliest part of the book contained the notion of an original island homeland near the earth's axis.[41] The Ko-ji-ki begins with the "Seven Generations of the Age of the Gods." Each "generation" consisted of a brother and sister. After all seven generations of siblings had been created, two more gods, Izanagi and his sister/wife Izanami, were brought into being. They were charged with the task of creating the world out of the porridge-like chaos that was the primordial earth. Warren summarizes the moment when the two celestial deities create the first world:

> . . . standing on the bridge of heaven, pushed down a spear into the green plain of the sea, and stirred it round and round. When they drew it up the drops which fell from its end consolidated onto an island. The sun-born pair descended onto the island, and planting a spear in the ground, point downwards, built a palace round it, taking that for the central roof-pillar. The spear became the axis

of the earth, which had been caused to revolve by stirring round.[42]

Warren concluded that Onogorojima ("Island of the Congealed Drop") was an island somewhere near the pole. The central "roof-pillar" represented, in his view, the earth's axis. A great palace was built on the island, a theme that reappears in the legend of Atlantis. (Later, Izanagi created other islands, including the eight main islands of Japan.)

But why would these people have made their home at the inhospitable pole? Warren answered that at the time the earth was much warmer, its temperature having only recently cooled. Heat was generated from within the planet and combined with surface temperatures to render tropical, and even temperate, lands far too hot to support life. Only the polar regions were cool enough at that time to invite human habitation.

Warren believed that the polar paradise was destroyed when a critical temperature drop resulted in a worldwide geological upheaval. A huge mass of the earth's interior collapsed inward, pulling sections of the planet's crust with it. The ocean rushed to drown the sunken areas. The globe then cooled — suffocating the original island paradise in snow and ice.

Because he believed that the entire island had disappeared beneath a polar ocean Warren dismissed the South Pole as a possible location since the Antarctic continent still existed as land. Instead, he focused his attention on the Arctic Ocean, which to him represented the true "Navel of the Earth":

> Students of antiquity must often have marveled that in nearly every ancient literature they should encounter the strange expression "the Navel of the Earth". Still more unaccountable would it have seemed to them had they noticed how many ancient mythologies *connect the cradle of the human race with this earth-navel*. The advocates of the different sites which have been assigned to Eden have seldom, if ever, recognised the fact that no hypothesis on this subject can be considered acceptable which cannot account for this peculiar association of man's first home

with some sort of natural centre of the earth. (italics in original)[43]

Warren believed that the "Navel of the Earth" referred to the earth's axis. His map of the location of the lost paradise depicts the earth as it appears from the North Pole. (See Map 7.)

If Warren hadn't been so fixed on the northern view and had instead looked to the south he would have seen that Antarctica represents a far more natural "Navel of the Earth," as we can see in a U.S. Navy map of the world as seen from Antarctica (see Map 8).

Antarctica sits, like the mythological homeland of the Okanagan, in the "middle of the ocean." Like the Aztec's "Aztlan," Antarctica is "white." Like Iran's lost paradise, Antarctica is covered "with a thick sheet of ice." And like the "first land" of Japanese mythology, it is

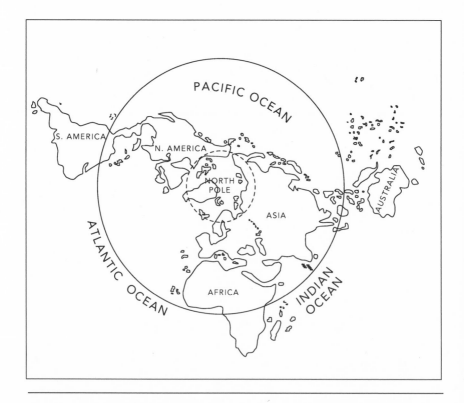

Map 7: Dr. William Fairfield Warren placed the mythological "Navel of the Earth" in the Arctic Ocean. He believed that this spot was the site of the lost island paradise.

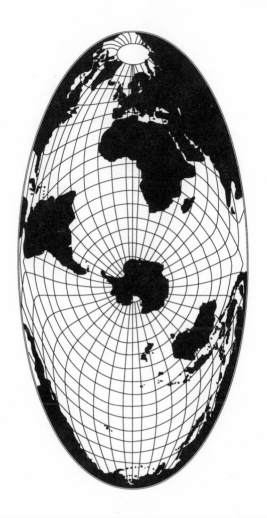

Map 8: A U.S. Navy map of the world depicting Antarctica in the centre of the ocean reveals the island continent as the natural "Navel of the Earth."

close to one of the earth's poles. This last-explored continent may well have been the lost island paradise of world mythology.

But how did people first arrive on Antarctica and how did it become a land forgotten?

Chapter Six
A Land Forgotten

Seen from space, our planet is a tiny turquoise jewel in a midnight black setting. But one landmass stands out from most of the others — the shining snow-covered continent of Antarctica. It is a mysterious and hostile place where few humans dare to venture.

Lesser Antarctica

Greater Antarctica

United States at the same scale

Map 9: The island continent of Antarctica is comparable in size to the lower forty-eight states of the United States. Geographers separate the continent into "Lesser" and "Greater" Antarctica.

Cold, nightless summers fade into colder, sunless winters. And always there is the wind, the constant howling wind of a land forgotten.

Antarctica's massive bulk covers an area greater than the lower forty-eight states of the United States. Most of our planet's fresh water is locked in Antarctica's ice cap. This vast ice sheet conceals a puzzle and, at the same time, provides a clue to the revolutions that sometimes uproot the foundations of the earth.

Geographers distinguish between "Lesser" and "Greater" Antarctica (see Map 9).

Lesser Antarctica, the "tail" that points towards South America, is characterized by its mountains, its thin ice sheet, and its heavy snowfall. Greater Antarctica, the "body" of the continent, holds most of the world's ice, even though it is now a polar desert. This ice sheet

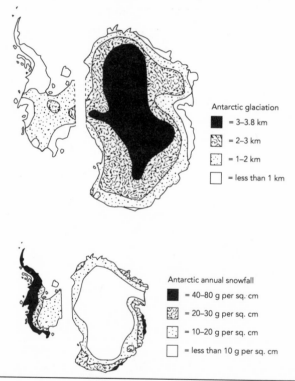

Antarctic glaciation

■ = 3–3.8 km
▨ = 2–3 km
▫ = 1–2 km
□ = less than 1 km

Antarctic annual snowfall

■ = 40–80 g per sq. cm
▨ = 20–30 g per sq. cm
▫ = 10–20 g per sq. cm
□ = less than 10 g per sq. cm

Map 10a & 10b: Today's climate cannot account for the shape of the Antarctic ice sheet. Lesser Antarctica has the least ice but the most annual snowfall, while Greater Antarctica holds the most ice yet experiences the least snowfall.

is over two miles thick, yet receives hardly any annual snowfall. This disparity between the present amount of annual snowfall of both Lesser and Greater Antarctica and the thickness of ice sheets demonstrates that Antarctica's climate must have been radically different in the past. (See Maps 10a and 10b.)

If we look at the northern hemisphere, it reveals a mirror image of the south. Central Greenland, like Greater Antarctica, is heavily glaciated.

Each spot on the earth's surface has an "antipodal" point, that is, a point exactly on the opposite side of the planet. If a line is drawn through one point on the earth, through the exact centre of the earth, that line will emerge at its antipodal point. The North Pole is antipodal to the South Pole. England and New Zealand are antipodal. North America and the southern part of the Indian Ocean lie on opposite sides of the earth. Greenland, covered with the largest ice sheet in the northern hemisphere, is very close to being antipodal to the great ice cap on Greater Antarctica. The area of thickest ice on Greenland overlaps the area of thickest ice on Antarctica. In every case, the points that are antipodal share the same amount of annual sunshine and thus similar temperatures.

Like its cousin to the south, Greenland's current snowfall does not match its ice cap. (See Maps 11a and 11b.)

The current climate cannot possibly account for the ice sheets on Greenland and Antarctica, and yet there has not been any explanation for this "odd" placement of the ice sheets. The problem is ignored. The present largest ice sheets are antipodal yet lopsided relative to the earth's axis. This suggests a displacement of the earth's crust — to be expected when lands shift in and out of the polar regions.

Earth crust displacement does, in fact, provide an answer to the problem. As the earth's crust shifts, it moves through the climatic zones. Some lands that had enjoyed mild climates before the shift were dragged into the polar zones. As a result, they received more snow. Other lands were released from the polar zones as they were shifted into warmer climates, causing their ice sheets to melt. Greenland and Greater Antarctica were locked into the polar zones before *and* after the displacement. Since these lands experienced

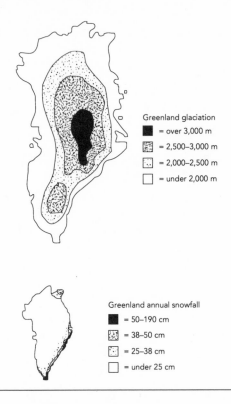

Greenland glaciation
■ = over 3,000 m
▨ = 2,500–3,000 m
▤ = 2,000–2,500 m
☐ = under 2,000 m

Greenland annual snowfall
■ = 50–190 cm
▨ = 38–50 cm
▤ = 25–38 cm
☐ = under 25 cm

Maps 11a & 11b: Like Antarctica, the shape of Greenland's ice sheet cannot be explained by present snowfall patterns. Greenland holds such immense amounts of ice because it has remained within the Arctic Circle both before and after the last two earth crust displacements.

polar conditions longer than any other parts of the world, they accumulated the greatest ice sheets. The overlapping old and new Arctic and Antarctic circles (it's actually the crust that moves, not the polar zones) leave the old ice sheets intact.

Until 9600 B.C., Lesser Antarctica was outside the polar zone. This area has hardly been explored for two reasons. First, three nations (Argentina, Chile, and the United Kingdom) all lay claim to it. No system of law has been established and territorial disputes overlap. Second, most scientists focus on studying Greater Antarctica's vast ice sheet. Because of limited data about the area of the continent that is most important to the mystery of Atlantis we must gauge Lesser Antarctica's past climate using the antipodal argument.

If we were to peer through a glass globe at the South Pole, aligning it with the North Pole, we could see those parts of the earth's crust that are opposite to Antarctica. These lands have been extensively studied (see Map 12).

In the summer of 1993, two Norwegian scientists were undertaking research in Arctic Norway. At a site 250 kilometres *north* of the Arctic Circle, zoologists Rolv Lie and Stein-Erik Lauritzen discovered polar bear bones dating to the last Ice Age. The finding was startling because geologists assume that Arctic Norway was under

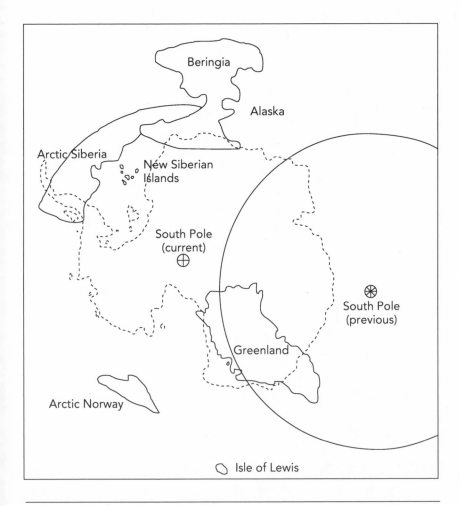

Map 12: Recent scientific investigations of Arctic Norway, the Scottish Isle of Lewis, Arctic Alaska, Beringia, and Arctic Siberia all point to a warmer climate during the last Ice Age. This raises the possibility that the corresponding areas of Lesser Antarctica could have enjoyed a mild climate before the earth crust displacement of 9600 B.C.

a vast ice cap from eighty to ten thousand years ago, making it impossible for any life to survive. The bones were not supposed to be there! Carbon-14 and uranium dating confirmed that the bones must be at least forty-two thousand years old. Further excavations revealed the remains of wolf, field mice, ants, and tree pollen.

"The wolf needs large prey like reindeer," said Lie. Reindeer, in turn, must be able to graze on bare ground. "The summers must have been relatively warm and the winters not excessively cold . . . the area wasn't under an icecap as we believed . . . "[1]

The existence of these animals and the plants upon which they depended challenges common notions about the last Ice Age. How could an area that was supposedly frozen in the polar zone exhibit characteristics only found in much warmer climates?

These difficulties disappear when we surrender the presupposition of a stable crust. If we treat the earth's crust as something that can change position relative to the North and South poles, then we can easily imagine reindeer, wolves, and ants living in an area that today cannot sustain them.

But the Norwegian discovery was not the only evidence that would challenge our assumption about the Arctic before 9600 B.C. Off the northwest coast of Scotland lies the remote Isle of Lewis. In 1984, two scientists made the amazing discovery that it was unglaciated between thirty-seven and twenty-three thousand years ago. They wrote:

> Models of the last ice sheet showing Scottish ice extending to the continental shelf edge depict the north of Lewis as being covered by 1,000–1,500 meters of ice, but our evidence demonstrates that part of this area was actually ice-free.[2]

When we shift our gaze to Arctic America, the evidence continues to build towards a new understanding of the world before 9600 B.C. In 1982, Dr. R. Dale Guthrie, at the Institute of Arctic Biology, was struck by the variety of animals in Alaska before 9600 B.C.:

> When learning of this exotic mixture of hyenas, mammoths, sabertooth cats, camels, horses, rhinos, asses,

deer with gigantic antlers, lions, ferrets, saiga and other Pleistocene species, one cannot help wondering about the world in which they lived. This great diversity of species, so different from that encountered today, raises the most obvious question: is it not likely that the rest of the environment was also different?[3]

As long as we assume that the earth's crust has always been relatively stable in relation to its axis we will not be able to grasp the simple fact that Alaska's flora and fauna depict *temperate*, not polar, conditions.

A great deal of archaeological and geological work has been done in northern Alaska, the Bering Sea, and northeastern Siberia. This area is of vital importance to the archaeological model of how people first arrived in the New World. The story begins in 1589 with Joseph de Acosta, a Jesuit missionary who had lived in Peru. He wrote *Historia natural moral de las Indies*, in which he pondered the question of the origins of the people and animals of America. His religion told him that Noah's ark was the only ship to have survived the Flood, but evidence from America pointed to another conclusion. Clearly, some people and animals had escaped the Flood and reached America. Acosta's faith in the Bible was so complete that he came to the conclusion that some descendants from Noah's ark must have reached America by way of a land-bridge either in the far south or far north.[4] His idea would come to bear fruit in the twentieth century, as we will shortly see.

In 1607 another writer, Gregorio Garcia, took a different approach. He assumed that shipbuilding was an ancient art that had survived Eden's destruction by the Great Flood: ". . . the art of navigation had been invented by Noah and was therefore as old as man."[5]

If ancient man could travel by sea, then perhaps the Aztec and Incan civilizations were offshoots of other civilizations. Egypt became the most popular "motherland" because the Egyptians had boats, built pyramids, and worshipped the sun as did the people of Mexico and Peru. Perhaps it served to rationalize the brutal plundering of the American civilizations. If the Mexican and Incan civilizations owed their very existence to the Old World, then destroying them was not such a sin. What was given freely could be taken at will.

After a century of speculation about the "diffusion" of culture from the Old to the New World, an event occurred that permanently changed the common notion of how the original people arrived in America. In 1728, Vitus Bering, a Danish navigator serving the Russian Czar, Peter the Great, reached the northeast limit of the Asian continent. The discovery of the Bering Strait between Siberia and Alaska would eventually revolutionize the debate about the origins of native Americans. One could easily imagine the people of Siberia making their way in boats to Alaska and thus populating the New World. The Atlantic Ocean avenue to America was now effectively ruled out.

In the twentieth century, anthropologists and archaeologists discovered that a former land-bridge between Siberia and Alaska called "Beringia" might have been a route travelled by the original human populations of America. Boats were not even necessary to carry the Siberians to America. Acosta's idea of a land-bridge came into its own and eventually came to dominate the discussion of the peopling of America.

During the last Ice Age the world's ocean level was lower because more moisture was captured at the poles as snow and ice. Much of the planet's continental shelf was above sea level. Beringia was one of these areas.

Russian and American scientists have long argued about the condition of Beringia prior to 9600 B.C. The Russians claim that the area was a vast steppe, while the Americans argue that it was tundra. A steppe is a treeless plain supporting a wide variety of animals such as lions, zebra, and the whole menagerie associated with terrain such as that now found in East Africa. Tundra, on the other hand, is cold and barren with snow-swept plains supporting only a few animals, such as fox, polar bear, and arctic falcon. The Russians believe that the steppe appears to change to tundra as one moves from Siberia towards Alaska.[6] The former grassy flora of late Pleistocene Siberia has been compared with today's African savannah.[7] Of the thirty-four species known to have lived in Siberia before 9600 B.C., including mammoths, giant deer, cave hyena, and cave

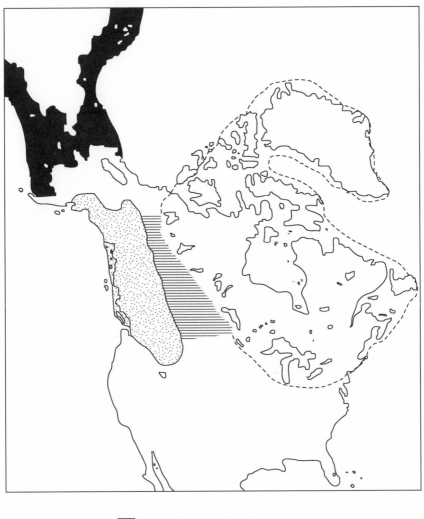

= ice-free corridor

= Cordilleran Ice Sheet

= Laurentide Ice Sheet

= Beringia

Map 13: Two vast ice sheets covered most of North America 11,600 years ago. The lower ocean level created a land-bridge called Beringia that connected a largely ice-free Alaska with an ice-free Siberia. Most archaeologists believe that people crossed into America from Asia over this land-bridge and then down an ice-free corridor between the two ice sheets.

lions, twenty-eight were adapted to temperate conditions.[8] As Cuvier realized, Siberia's climate must have been much warmer than it is today in order to have supported these animals. Two Russian scientists found the remains of saiga antelope (considered to be an indicator of steppe conditions) on the New Siberian Islands, which lie *north* of the Siberian Arctic mainland.[9] Charles Hapgood wrote of these now barren lands:

> There the remains of mammoths and other animals are most numerous of all. There Baron Toll, the Arctic explorer, found remains of a sabertooth tiger, and a fruit tree that had been ninety feet tall when it was standing.[10]

At the same time that "Arctic" Siberia was full of life and largely free of ice, two vast ice sheets bore down on North America. At its height the Laurentide Ice Sheet, centred on Hudson Bay, was larger than Antarctica's current ice cap. It covered most of Canada as well as the states that border the Great Lakes. In fact, the Great Lakes are the remnants of its force. In the west, the Cordilleran Ice Sheet lay along the Rocky Mountains, covering southern Alaska, almost all of British Columbia, and a good share of Alberta, Washington, Idaho, and Montana. When these two ice sheets melted, Beringia was flooded. At this time, an *ice-free corridor* between the ice sheets served as a trail for the travellers from Asia to cross into America (see Map 13).

Although the existence of the ice-free corridor has been accepted by archaeologists, it has never been explained. Why should this region be ice-free? Hapgood supplies a simple answer: the crust was in a different position when the corridor was formed. The sun would rise from the direction of the Gulf of Mexico and set towards the Yukon. This arc of sunshine cut a path through the ice and melted the snow that fell there. The appearance of the ice-free corridor is no longer so "odd."

As we have seen, earth crust displacement can also explain the formation and demise of the world's former ice sheets and, at the same time (and for the first time), account for today's ice sheets on Greenland and Antarctica. Now our focus will be to show why the former locations of the earth's crust account for current and past ice sheets.

●

Prior to 91,600 B.C. the crust was situated in such a way that Canada's Yukon Territory stood at the North Pole. The Arctic Circle of this time encompassed most of the northwestern half of North America, as well as all of Alaska, Beringia, and much, but not all, of northeastern Siberia (see Map 14).

This arrangement of the crust accounts for the Cordilleran Ice Sheet. During this era, passage from Asia to America was completely blocked. Europe was warmer than it is today and Greenland was without ice.

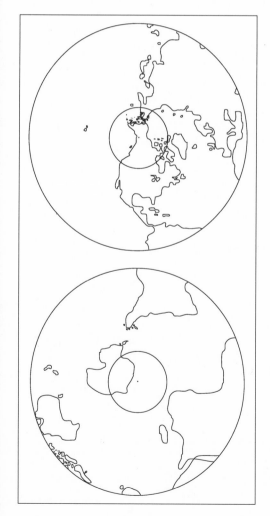

Map 14: Before 91,600 B.C., the Arctic Circle was centred on the northwest corner of North America. In the south, that part of Greater Antarctica that lies towards Africa was under ice. Much of Lesser Antarctica was ice-free.

An earth crust displacement at 91,600 B.C. moved the crust so that Europe fell within the Arctic Circle. (See Map 15.)

From 91,600 B.C. to 50,600 B.C., Europe and Greenland were smothered under ice. In the south, much of Greater Antarctica remained encapsulated in ice. Passage to America from Asia, across Beringia, was possible sometime after the old Alaskan ice cap melted. This means that people from Asia might have arrived in America before 50,600 B.C., an idea that has recently gained archaeological support.

In the March 1994 issue of *Popular Science*, Ray Nelson reported on an important archaeological finding in New Mexico. Dr. Richard S.

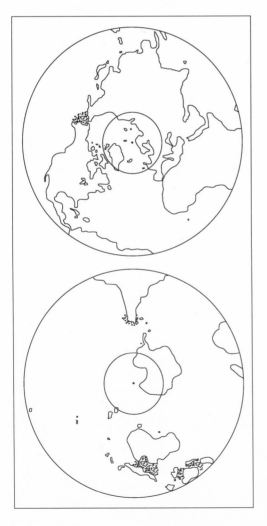

Map 15: Between 50,600 and 91,600 B.C. the Arctic Circle contained much of Europe and all of Greenland. Passage from Asia to America was open. Northeastern Siberia, Beringia, and Alaska enjoyed a mild climate. In the south, the part of Greater Antarctica leaning towards New Zealand was under ice.

MacNeish, along with his team from the Andover Foundation for Archaeological Research, excavated a site at Pendejo Cave, in southwestern New Mexico. They found, in a cave about 100 metres above the desert, eleven human hairs. Radiocarbon dating placed the evidence at 55,000 years ago.[11]

An earth crust displacement at 50,600 B.C. moved the crust again, this time bringing North America into the polar zone. (See Map 16.)

The Arctic Circle now lay over Hudson Bay rather than the "Arctic" Ocean.

People and animals from Siberia could have crossed Beringia into Alaska and then moved *east* along the Pacific coast all the way to

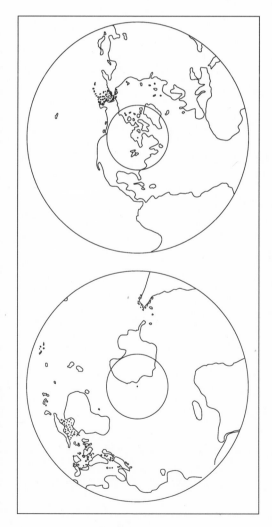

Map 16: Between 50,600 and 9600 B.C. North America felt the grip of the Arctic Circle. The massive Laurentide Ice Sheet was created during this time. Lesser Antarctica, like Siberia, Beringia, and Alaska, was ice-free except in the high mountains. During this time Asians could have easily arrived in the New World and even made their way to an ice-free Lesser Antarctica.

California. This Pacific waterway to America was open and inviting.[12] It would have been possible for seafarers to travel along the coasts of Alaska and British Columbia to Washington without enduring many adjustments to their hunting and gathering way of life. And once they got to North America it would have been possible to get to South America and then to an ice-free Lesser Antarctica. If this were the case, then people could have been living on Lesser Antarctica, in the antipodal areas to Arctic Norway, northern Alaska, Beringia, and Siberia. They may have lived there anywhere from 50,600 B.C. to 9600 B.C. (or longer). (See Map 17.)

However, after the earth crust displacement of 9600 B.C., the people of Lesser Antarctica (Atlantis) would have had to flee their homeland as the Antarctic Circle encapsulated the whole island (see Map 18).

After the displacement of 9600 B.C., the ice sheet centred on Hudson Bay began to melt. Beringia was submerged by the rising

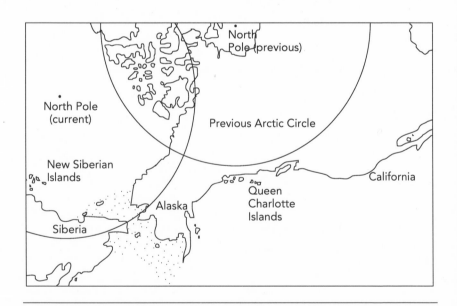

Map 17: Directions change with each earth crust displacement. Before the last catastrophe, the Pacific side of North America was actually the *south* coast, while the Arctic Circle was centred on Hudson Bay. Seen from this perspective, the migration of people from Siberia, across Beringia, and along the Pacific coast would be a movement from *west* to *east*.

level of the world's ocean as the old ice caps added water to the seas. Alaska and Siberia's climate took a dramatic turn for the worse.

It is assumed that people trapped in Alaska and unable to return to Siberia were forced south, and that these "first" Americans arrived through the "ice-free corridor" after 9600 B.C. There is very little archaeological evidence to support this theory. One possibility that is not considered is the one that most closely matches the tales told by the people themselves: that they came from a white island destroyed by a great flood. They regarded their island as "white" because two-thirds of Antarctica was under snow.

The origins of the people of America are probably mixed. Some, no doubt, did arrive from Asia after 9600 B.C. Others, however, might

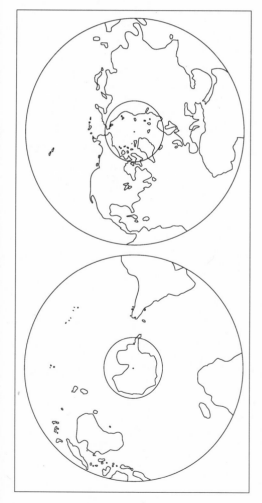

Map 18: An earth crust displacement 11,600 years ago created the current placement of the Arctic and Antarctic circles. Siberia, Alaska, and northern Norway are no longer inviting locations for settlement. Lesser Antarctica, the site of Atlantis, was destroyed not only by earthquakes and floods, but also by a dire winter that completely covered the achievements of a lost civilization.

have already been in America and Antarctica for forty thousand or even eighty thousand years before this time.

All of our recorded advancements, from the first experiments with agriculture shortly after 9600 B.C., to the Space Age, have occurred in less than twelve thousand years. Forty to eighty thousand years would seem to be more than enough time to create an advanced civilization on a temperate island free from external invasion.

As noted earlier, in 1552, Francisco Lopez de Gomara, Cortes's secretary, wrote that native Americans said they had come from the lost island of Aztlan, which he believed was Plato's lost continent of Atlantis. After 1589, with the publication of Acosta's theory of a land-bridge, the Atlantis theory fell out of favour. When the former existence of Beringia was confirmed, the Atlantis theory, as an explanation for the origins of native Americans, died completely in the journals of science. Archaeologists turned more to the idea of exploration/adventure as a model for the peopling of America. They took the European experience of conquest and created a forced interpretation of the natives' history. The original people, we are told, were earlier pioneers seeking a new and better land. This simple projection of the European experience is not even remotely close to the tales told by native Americans themselves.

Theirs is a story of catastrophic displacement from an island paradise by a great flood.

A story of survival in an alien land.

A story told all over the world, not just in America.

A story best known as "Atlantis."

Chapter Seven

From Atlantis

It began on a morning like any other. Steam rose from the swamps and bogs of the tropics. Clouds of mist covered the quiet lakes of Africa. Only a faint rustle across the grasslands betrayed the presence of the morning's first breeze. But on this day the silence was to be broken by a sound and a trembling that filled the earth with alarm. A rumbling slowly turned to a roar as the earth's foundations were uprooted.

The beat of hundreds of thousands of wings brushed the sky as flocks of birds rose from their nests to seek safety. Herds of roaming creatures raised their huge heads from their foraging and sniffed and shuffled restlessly with a strange unease. As the terrifying roar began to deafen them and the undulations of the earth triggered a deep panic, the wild herds began to run, desperately seeking shelter from the coming catastrophe. Terror struck the hearts of men and women as they flung themselves to their knees, pleading with their gods to spare them. But no mercy was to be shown. The earth's revolt would crush them all, wrenching all living things from their homes.

Earthquakes of extraordinary violence strained the very foundations of the earth. At the polar caps, mountains of ice began to crumble and dissolve. The din became unbearable as great avalanches of ice were shaken loose from their precarious perches and slid into a relentlessly rising sea.

Unchained, the ocean spilled from the confines of its gigantic basin. It gathered all its mighty force and began a slow, inevitable roll to the shore. Gaining speed and power, the unrestrained wave raced with the turning earth to overwhelm defenceless shores.

The earth itself was an active performer in the tragedy. The sliding crust was the unseen instigator of the ocean's wild rebellion. Beneath the sand and rocks of the ocean floor, the earth's crust buckled like an angry horse ridding itself of a dreaded rider.

Tidal wave followed tidal wave as earthquakes broke new ground along the ocean floor. Rivers overflowed as gales of rain relentlessly pounded the earth. A flood, a deluge, a storm, and a hell — the likes of which no living human had seen — plagued the planet as the world's ocean broke its boundaries.

Slowly the water began to die down, the roar of the earth subsided, and the sun once again rose on a silent world. But it was not a silence of peace. It carried with it the ominous quiet of the slow and deadly process of freezing. A third disaster was preparing to strike opposite areas of the globe.

In Siberia the reign of the great ivory-tusked, shaggy-haired mammoths came to a sudden end. The lush grasslands that had provided them with a bountiful living disappeared as snow began to fall. When it was over, Siberia had been transformed from a country that could support the voracious appetites of mammoths to a land whose very name would come to be synonymous with desolation.

The deadly process was not confined to the animals of Siberia. On the other side of the globe, in Lesser Antarctica, a veil of snow and ice was drawn across the land. As each century added yet more snow, the history of the people who once lived there began to fade.

The Atlanteans perished in such an overwhelming catastrophe that the fruits of their long and profound history were torn to shreds by the upheaval of the earth, drowned by the force of its ocean, and, finally, locked deep in the recesses of a grave of ice. Atlantis was lost as the world's ocean swept across the globe. But a great legend had begun.

We first learn of Atlantis and its destruction in the writings of Plato. He assures us that the history of Atlantis is ". . . a tale which, though passing strange, is yet wholly true, as Solon, the wisest of the Seven, once affirmed."[1] Solon (c. 638–559 B.C.) was one of the seven acknowledged wise men of ancient Greece.

Solon earned his fame as the founder of Athenian democracy when that city was facing a severe crisis. At the time, Athens's population was suffering from an unhealthy split between the few rich and the heavily indebted poor. The famous Roman biographer, Plutarch (c. 46–c. 120 A.D.), describes the situation leading to the appointment of Solon as that city's lawgiver:

> The city stood on the brink of revolution, and it seemed as if the only way to put a stop to its perpetual disorders and achieve stability was to set up a tyranny . . . At this point the most level-headed of the Athenians began to look towards Solon. They saw that he, more than anyone else, stood apart from the injustices of the time and was involved neither in the exortations of the rich nor the privations of the poor, and so finally they appealed to him to come forward and settle their differences.[2]

Because he took exclusive power from the aristocrats and alleviated the debts of the poor, Solon is regarded as the founder of Athenian democracy and as such the forefather of all democracies. His concern for freedom and his compassion for the poor led him to question long-ingrained injustices. Serfdom and slavery for debt were abolished and the use of personal freedom as a pledge against loans was outlawed. We once again turn to Plutarch for the most precise telling of the unusual chain of events:

> Once Solon's laws had been put into effect, people came to visit him every day, praising some of them and finding fault with others, or advising him to insert a certain provision here or take out another there. A great many wanted to ask questions and cross-examine him on points of detail, and they kept pressing him to explain what was the object of this or that regulation. Solon saw that it was out of the question to meet such demands, but also that he would earn great ill-will if he turned them all down. He was anxious to disengage himself from these complications and thus escape the fault-finding and the captious criticism of his fellow countrymen, for as he remarks

himself, "In great affairs you cannot please all parties." So he made his commercial interests as a shipowner an excuse to travel and sailed away obtaining leave of absence for ten years from the Athenians, in the hope that during this period they would become accustomed to his laws. He went first of all to Egypt . . .[3]

Why Egypt? For the ancient Greeks, Egypt was the fountain of knowledge, and as was the case with so many Greeks, Solon had a thirst for knowledge. To travel to Egypt, no matter what the hardships involved, was a necessary journey for those seeking wisdom. Solon was by no means the only philosophical pilgrim who wished to learn from the priests of Egypt. Clustered around the searing sand at the base of the pyramids were not the empty looted vaults of past pharaohs, which now meet our gaze, but instead a thriving community, wise with age and in possession of a wealth of written information controlled by a powerful group of priests.

At times, the Egyptian priests even challenged the Pharaoh. Religion permeated every action, thought, and deed. The priests were more than mere caretakers of ritual, they were astronomers, mathematicians, civic administrators, and guardians of the secret sciences of antiquity. Only the brightest children could enter the priesthood, and if they were fortunate, after a very long period of study and devotion, a handful were chosen to see the most sacred texts. Solon sought out these priests and their access to the secrets of the past. Plutarch tells of this stage in Solon's quest:

> He spent some time studying and discussing philosophy with Psenophis of Heliopolis and Sonchis of Sais, who were the most learned of the Egyptian priests. According to Plato it was from them that he heard the legend of the lost continent of Atlantis . . .[4]

What we do know of the location of Atlantis is voiced by the Egyptian priest whom Plutarch identifies as Sonchis.

The question arises as to why Sonchis would freely give the precious secrets of Egypt to a foreigner, no matter how esteemed he was. Solon and the Greeks, however, were not regarded as foreigners.

Sonchis explained that the Greeks and Egyptians were once brothers who shared the same mother goddess. Sonchis told Solon:

> . . . I begrudge you not the story, Solon; nay, I will tell it,
> both for your own sake and that of your city, and most of
> all for the sake of the Goddess who had adopted for her
> own both your land and this of ours . . . And the duration
> of our civilization as set down in our sacred writings is
> 8000 years. Of the citizens, then, who lived 9000 years ago,
> I will declare to you briefly certain of their laws and the
> noblest of the deeds they performed: the full account in
> precise order and detail we shall go through later at our
> leisure, taking the actual writings.[5]

The high priest then revealed the history of the Atlantean civilization and its destruction nine thousand years before by "earthquakes and floods of extraordinary violence." He emphasized that
the entire globe was shaken by these traumatic geological events.
This conversation took place around 560 B.C., thus placing the fall
of Atlantis at approximately 9560 B.C., a date that corresponds
directly with the last earth crust displacement. At a time when most
of North America was buried under a vast ice sheet, an area of
Antarctica the size of Western Europe was *ice-free*. Before the earth's
crust shifted, these ice-free regions could have supported Atlantis.

The Egyptian priest attempted to explain to Solon the nature and
location of Atlantis, but in order to give an accurate account he had
to reach beyond the Greeks' limited notion of the globe. His description contains sixteen clues to the site of the lost land.

The Egyptian Priest's Clues to Atlantis[6]

1. 9560 B.C.
2. change in the path of the sun
3. worldwide earthquakes of extraordinary violence
4. overwhelming worldwide floods
5. island
6. continent (larger than Libya and Asia)
7. high above sea level

8. numerous high mountains
9. impressive cliffs rising sharply from the ocean
10. other islands
11. abundant mineral resources
12. beyond the Pillars of Heracles (known world)
13. in a distant point in the "Atlantic" ocean
14. in the "real ocean"
15. the Mediterranean Sea is only a bay of the real ocean
16. the true continent completely surrounds the real ocean

Plato's description of its location depicts the world as a native of Atlantis would see it. The world of 9600 B.C. seen *from* the shores of Antarctica appeared much different than it does to a citizen of the twentieth century. (Each culture's unique filter brings a different perspective to the globe. For example, in China the homeland was called the *Middle Kingdom* and yet the Europeans considered China as part of the *Far East*. One nation's centre is inevitably another's periphery.)

Our current European-centred notion of the planet is the direct result of the history of the age of exploration. The prejudices of European explorers became the world's prejudices. Even the common divisions of east and west are only relative to Europe. But there is no *geographic* reason to place Europe in the centre of the world. Our planet is quite democratically round.

The Greeks of Solon's time saw the world as an island in the middle of a vast ocean. This world-island was divided into three important cultural units: Europe, Libya, and Asia. (See Map 19.)

The ancient Greeks believed that "Libya" covered the area we now call "North Africa." Their "Asia" is equivalent to our present-day "Middle East." Only "Europe" matches its contemporary area.

At the western extreme of the Greeks' world lay the "Pillars of Heracles," a description that has *two* meanings. The expression refers to the specific location, the Strait of Gibraltar, but also to the *extremity of the known world*. The Greek poet Pindar (518–438 B.C.) wrote that the Pillars of Heracles were considered ". . . the farthest limits [of the Greek world] . . . What lies beyond cannot be trodden by the wise or unwise."[7]

94

Map 19: The Greeks of Solon's time believed that the world was a disc floating on an ocean of water. The island was divided into Europe, Libya (North Africa), and Asia (the Middle East).

The Pillars of Heracles were a psychological barrier, a forbidden gateway beyond which none but the foolish would dare to venture. This meaning of the "Pillars of Heracles" is often forgotten or ignored by searchers for Atlantis who assume only a literal interpretation of the words, thereby limiting the location of the lost continent to the North Atlantic Ocean. This mistake is compounded when they examine the "Atlantic Ocean."

Plato's Egyptian priest places Atlantis at ". . . a distant point in the Atlantic Ocean." But what did "Atlantic Ocean" mean to the ancient Greeks? Aristotle defined it as a body of water that completely surrounded the world-island: "The sea, which is outside our inhabited earth, and washes our region all round is called both 'Atlantic' and 'the ocean.'"[8]

The ancient Greek view of the "Atlantic Ocean" as being the only ocean in the world started to slip from our understanding when the explorers of the late fifteenth and early sixteenth centuries began their travels. As they sailed around Africa and South America, charting the unknown sea and seeking routes to exotic treasures, they renamed parts of the ocean. After a dangerous voyage through treacherous straits off South America, Ferdinand Magellan (c.1480–1521) finally reached a calm and open sea, which, in his relief, he named the "Pacific Ocean," meaning "Peaceful" ocean. Similarly, Vasco da Gama (c.1460–1524) christened the route that took him to India the "Indian Ocean."

The prospect of navigating an unknown and overwhelming ocean was made a little less terrifying by dividing it into manageable sections (no matter how artificial), which could then be plotted on the explorers' newly drawn maps. Soon the clamour for spices, silk, and other precious Asian goods created a demand for even more detailed charts of ocean trade routes. These maps reinforced the false concept of a divided ocean, thereby effectively erasing the original Greek meaning of the term "Atlantic Ocean." "Atlantic" came to denote that body of water west of Europe and east of North and South America. The mistaken conclusion that the lost continent must have been west of the Pillars of Heracles in the North Atlantic Ocean has restricted the search for Atlantis to a mere fraction of the area that the Greeks defined as the "Atlantic Ocean."

●

Unlike our ancestors, who had to sail their way around the globe in a patchwork fashion, we are able to see the entire planet through the eye of a satellite. This view from space offers a fresh perspective on the earth's geography.

From a European-centred view there are seven continents and five oceans. However, photographs from space reveal that these classifications are unrelated to the true geographic contours of the planet. Europe is merely a peninsula of the Afro-Euro-Asian continent and North and South America are actually one continuous land mass separated only by the man-made Panama Canal. Treating North and South America as separate continents served the interests of the kings and queens of Portugal, Spain, and England, not the science of geography. And what is true of the continents is also true of the "oceans."

Our habitual view of the planet depicting north at the "top" of the globe reinforces the appearance of the ocean being separated into several bodies of water. However, oceanographers have long realized that our planet has only one ocean — the "World Ocean."

> The concept of the World Ocean held by a marine scientist is somewhat different than that of the layman. All of us learn in grade school to identify the names and placement of the continents and oceans. This exercise reveals that the oceans completely surround the land mass, but it is slightly misleading because it suggests that the oceans are separated geographically. From an oceanographer's point of view, the emphasis should be on a world ocean that is completely intercommunicating.[9]

The unity of the single World Ocean can be easily seen when the planet is viewed from the southern hemisphere as it is in this U.S. Navy map (see Map 20) of the world centred on Antarctica.

When viewed from Antarctica, the World Ocean is ringed by a super-continent comprised of Afro-Euro-Asia and the American

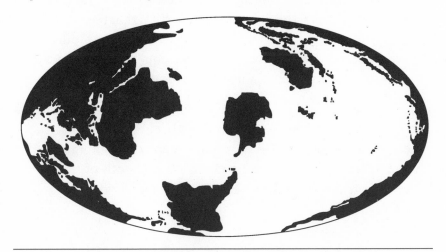

Map 20: When we place Antarctica in the centre of a world map, the Atlantic, Pacific, and Indian oceans appear as one body of water. This is what oceanographers call the "World Ocean."

landmasses. As we have seen, when Atlantis existed North and South America were connected to Afro-Euro-Asia by a land-bridge called "Beringia." Together they formed a "World Continent" that, from the perspective of Antarctica, encircled the World Ocean.

Sonchis told Solon that the Greeks themselves had a myth that was even older than the Flood. Sonchis mocked the Greeks' sparse knowledge of the past:

> O Solon, Solon, you Greeks are always children: there is not such a thing as an old Greek . . . You possess not a single belief that is ancient and derived from old tradition, nor yet one science that is hoary with age.[10]

He described events that happened immediately *before* the Flood:

> . . . many and manifold are the destructions of mankind that have been and shall be; the greatest are by fire and water; but besides these there are lesser ones in countless other fashions. Your own story of how Phaethon, the child of the Sun, yoked his father's chariot, and because he was unable to drive it along his father's path, burnt up things on the earth and himself was smitten by a thunderbolt and slain is a mythical version of the truth that there is at long intervals a deviation of the bodies that move around the earth in the heavens and consequent widespread destruction by fire of things on the earth.[11]

To save humankind, Zeus destroyed Phaethon with a thunderbolt and then unleashed the Flood to put out the fire. This "story" traces precisely the sequence of events that would erupt during an earth crust displacement. A shocking change in the path of the sun is followed by violent worldwide earthquakes and floods.

The priest's description of Atlantis's geography is amazingly detailed. The actual size of Antarctica closely matches that of North Africa ("Libya") and the Middle East ("Asia") combined. The Egyptian lived six centuries before the birth of Christ, yet he accurately described the geographic attributes of a continent undiscovered until the nineteenth century and not fully explored until the second half of the twentieth century.

Geologists, using the theory of plate tectonics, have concluded that Antarctica was once joined to the mineral-rich lands of South Africa, Western Australia, and South America, and so similar mineral resources must be locked beneath its frozen soil.

Two of the geological clues could only have been confirmed by modern science. In 1958 it was discovered that Antarctica, contrary to what we see on most modern maps, is not a monolithic landmass, but rather an island continent adjoined by a group of smaller islands not visible to the naked eye. Although these neighbouring islands are covered by a fresh ice cap, seismic surveys have penetrated their blanket of snow to reveal the true shape of the island continent. An ice-free map of Antarctica unveils the "other islands" mentioned in Plato's account (see Map 21).

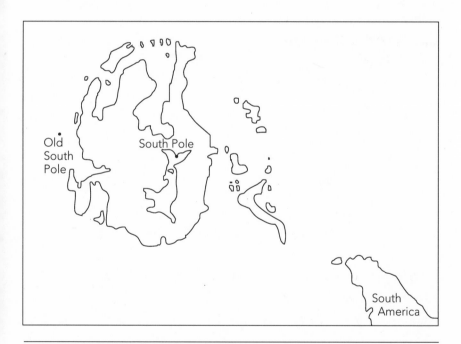

Map 21: Without its cover of ice, Antarctica is revealed as an island adjoined by a series of smaller islands that are scattered towards South America.

The priest told Solon:

> To begin with the region as a whole was said to be high above the level of the sea, from which it rose precipitously . . . [and the mountains] were celebrated as being more numerous, higher and more beautiful than any that exist today . . .[12]

Whitaker's Almanack (1992) gives the following description of the geology of Antarctica:

> The most conspicuous physical features of the continent are its high inland plateau (much of it over 10,000 ft.), the Transantarctic Mountains . . . and the mountainous Antarctic Peninsula and off-lying islands. The continental shelf averages 20 miles in width (half the global mean, and in places it is non-existent) . . .[13]

Like Atlantis, Antarctica is high above sea level; indeed it is the highest continent in the world:

Average Elevation in Feet[14]

Antarctica	6,500
Asia	3,200
South America	2,000
Africa	2,000
North America	1,900
Europe	940
Australia	800

Plato's account provides an accurate, global view of the world as described to a Greek with a limited view of the earth. Although different from our current perspective, it is accurate if we imagine ourselves residents of Antarctica. Atlantis is described to the Greek as being beyond his known world (Pillars of Heracles), and encircled by a vast body of water called the "real" ocean. Compared to the real ocean, the Mediterranean Sea is ". . . but a bay having a narrow entrance." The real ocean was the World Ocean. Plato's chronicle

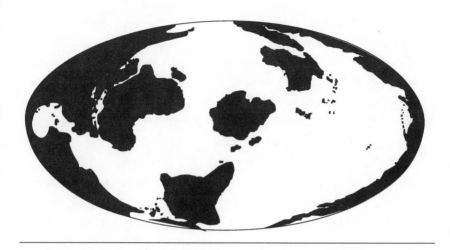

Map 22: The Atlantean World View of 9600 B.C. The Atlanteans saw the world like a dart board with Atlantis as the bull's eye. The World Ocean formed an inner ring of water. The rest of the earth formed an outer ring, the world continent. This outer continent included South America,

states that, when seen from Atlantis, the "real ocean" appeared to be framed by an unbroken mass of land that "may with fullest truth and fitness be named a continent."[15]

The map above reconstructs this ancient world view (see Map 22). It shows the Earth as seen from Antarctica before the last earth crust displacement and the catastrophic destruction of Atlantis. Due to lower ocean levels at the time, England and Japan were not islands and Beringia joined the Americas with the Afro-Euro-Asian continent, forming the unbroken World Continent.

The high priest of Egypt says that Atlantis was an island beyond the known world in a distant point in the Atlantic. It was:

> . . . larger than Libya and Asia combined; from it there was passage for the sea-farers of those times to reach the other islands, and from them the whole opposite continent which surrounds what can truly be called the ocean. For these regions that lie within the strait we were talking about seem to be but a bay having a narrow entrance; but the other ocean is the real ocean and the land which entirely surrounds it may with fullest truth and fitness be named a continent.[16]

Every search for Atlantis is built upon the foundation of these two sentences spoken by an Egyptian priest twenty-five centuries ago. The priest claimed the location of Atlantis was recorded in Egypt's most ancient records, presumably originally written by a survivor of the lost land. When compared to Map 22, this Atlantean account of the earth becomes exactly what Plato claims: an accurate depiction of a real place at a very specific time.

After the catastrophe, torn and shattered, abandoned to a freezing death, Atlantis lived on with a strange fascination in the memories of peoples scattered throughout the globe. Shreds of the past and wisps of recollection were woven together over the centuries.

Remnants of this delicate fabric of history eventually came into the hands of the learned Egyptian priest, Sonchis. Many rare documents had no doubt passed through the hands of this honoured priest, but the story of Atlantis he carefully wrapped, sending it intact from generation to generation through the voice of Solon and, eventually, Plato.

All the clues to the whereabouts of the great city of Atlantis, like the clues to the location of the continent itself, are found in Plato's writings.

Cast your mind back, if you will, to a time almost twelve thousand years ago when the World Ocean was navigated by the sailors of the Atlantean Empire . . .[17]

•

The chill of the ocean wind stiffened his bones. His lips were cracked and sore from long months of exposure to bitter sea salt. But there was a gleam in his pale eyes as the sailor squinted across the ship's deck.

There she was, only a few hours' travel away, shining against the horizon, a vision he had only dimly seen in his dreams for all the months he'd toiled and done his duty at sea. Atlantis. The shining city. Capital of an empire. Home.

The mountains of the continent rose in defiance of the waves, reassuring him with the eternal lines that dominated the sky, the sea, and the land itself. The austere welcome of the rigorous peaks was softened by their beauty, reaching so high they seemed to invite a duel with the sun.

The last hours seemed interminable, but as the fleet drifted towards port the clamour from the harbour and the surrounding merchants' quarter was carried to the crew by the wind, long before they prepared to dock. The ceaseless din, the calls and demands of anxious traders, the cries of animals, and the clanging of wares were a sweet tune to the sailors of the colossal Atlantean fleet. From their pivotal location in the belly of the ocean, the Atlanteans had access to every corner of the world. But to the weary sailor, no land, however exotic or fascinating, could compare with Atlantis.

The buildings clustered on top of the forbidding outer wall were infused with the brilliance of the approaching sunset as the ship and crew began their familiar preparations to enter the first of the great canals that would guide them through a ten-kilometre route to the city centre. Pungent odours from bustling stalls gradually replaced the bracing air of the sea. The increasing din of the marketplace signalled a return to civilization as the monotony of the sea gave way to the frantic activity of the merchants' section poised atop the great wall.

The clamour and excitement were to be expected at the port of a capital as renowned as Atlantis. Here the distribution of the goods to sustain a vast empire kept this vital section of the city a scene of constant activity. Providing the lifeblood of the empire, the prospering merchants enveloped three-quarters of the outer city. Trade and barter hummed constantly as foreign fleets crowded the massive docks dominating the port.

These docks were an integral part of a fortress equal to any ever conceived. Built in defence of the Atlanteans' precious material and spiritual treasures, they were carved from the white, black, and red rock of the land itself. A masterpiece of ingenuity, their pattern was continued in the substance of the towers and gates guarding the entrance. The business conducted in this extensive, noisy section of the city was responsible in no small part for the prosperity and leisure enjoyed by all Atlanteans.

Noise from the market receded as the fleet entered the confines of the canal. Incoming ships were dwarfed by the cliffs that lined the canal, towering on either side. An intimidating welcome indeed to any foreigner. The ship and her anxious crew were now on their way to their final destination, the inner sanctum of the great capital itself. But in order to reach their haven the ships must travel a slow route through a complex series of canals (see Maps 23a and 23b).

The young sailor's impatience to reach its legendary centre was tempered by the comfort of being once again within the embrace of his home. His ancestors had constructed a capital befitting their reputation. The city of Atlantis was an incredible example of city planning on a scale that the twentieth century has yet to match. They used the most abundant and obvious of power sources — water — to serve their most important needs. Ironically, the forces of water were to write their epitaph. All the city's commercial and transportation needs were met by an intricate system of canals that

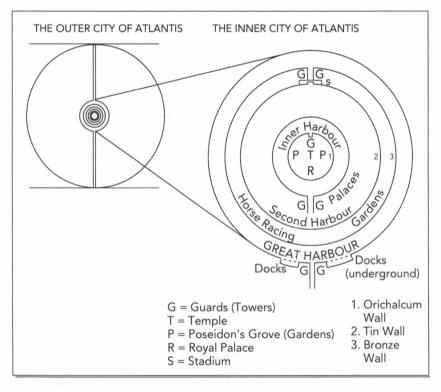

Maps 23a & 23b: The city of Atlantis consisted of rings of land that were, in turn, ringed by water. The inner city housed royalty, the gardens, racing tracks, palaces, and a temple. The outer city was populated by merchants and traders.

reached beyond the city into the great plain and further up to the very source of the bountiful waters, the mountains.

Not Rome, Alexandria, nor Constantinople, the capital of the Byzantine Empire, could outshine Atlantis for sheer size and beauty. In diameter alone, the city covered twenty-three kilometres. A massive carved wall, crowned with dwellings, traced a seventy-two-kilometre girth around the city. Most of London's famous sites would fit comfortably within the dimensions of the inner section of the city of Atlantis. And unlike the haphazard core of the United Kingdom's capital, Atlantis was a masterpiece of planning. (See Maps 24a and 24b.)

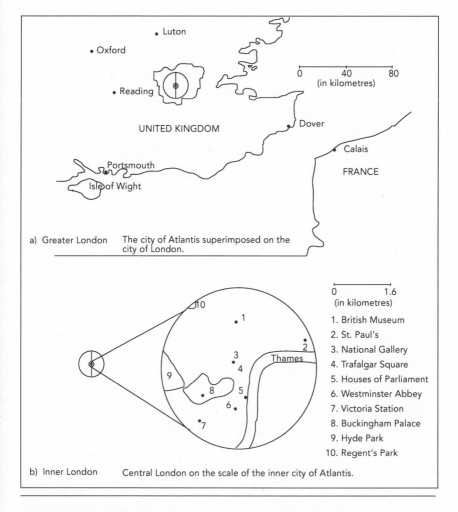

a) Greater London   The city of Atlantis superimposed on the city of London.

0   1.6
(in kilometres)

1. British Museum
2. St. Paul's
3. National Gallery
4. Trafalgar Square
5. Houses of Parliament
6. Westminster Abbey
7. Victoria Station
8. Buckingham Palace
9. Hyde Park
10. Regent's Park

b) Inner London   Central London on the scale of the inner city of Atlantis.

Maps 24a & 24b: The capital city of Atlantis was as large as modern-day London.

The towers and gates of outer Atlantis would have been fairly easy obstacles to overcome compared to what lay before any invader intent upon unveiling the mysteries of the inner city. Whether enemy or friend, no one could fail to be impressed as they sailed across the stretch of water half a kilometre wide (Map 23b) separating the inner city from the mercantile quarter. This expanse led to a shining wall of brass that concealed the only entrance to the inner city.

Once granted admittance, the full spectrum of the great civilization could be glimpsed. The first ring of land contained a racing stadium, gymnastic areas, and gardens blooming with exotic flowers, plants, and trees from around the world. Beyond this leisure area the pattern of water and land was repeated. The next belt of land was elevated and surrounded by a wall of tin. It protected the palaces, gardens, and fountains of the lesser noblemen of Atlantis.

And then, as if the Atlanteans had deliberately tempted any unwary traveller with the promise of ever more wonderful sights, the last belt of water girdled by still higher land came into view. This area was also surrounded by a wall, this time covered in "orichalcum," a metal unique to Atlantis that "sparkled like fire." It was from this central island, the pinnacle of the pyramid city of shining walls, that the Atlantean Empire was ruled.

On the central island the "Grove of Poseidon" surrounded the temple. Hot and cold water flowed through the gardens, providing cooling pools in the summer and warm baths in the winter. The temple and palace were protected by a gold-encrusted wall and the temple itself was coated with silver. Its interior was graced by statues, including a giant one depicting the god of the sea, "standing on a chariot," its reins connected to "six winged steeds." One hundred sea-nymphs astride dolphins accompanied the sea-god across the ocean.

At the altar of the temple of the ocean-god were enshrined the laws governing the ten princes of the ten provinces of Atlantis. They were engraved on a pillar of orichalcum and the king and princes would gather ". . . every fifth year, and then alternately every sixth year" to take part in an ancient ritual designed to renew their blood links. The first order of business was always the enforcement of the laws ". . . and when thus assembled they took counsel about public affairs and inquired if any had in any way transgressed and gave judgement."[18]

These intense deliberations were followed by elaborate rituals meant to reinforce the rulers' mutual commitment to the laws of Atlantis.

> When darkness came on and the sacrificial fire had died down, all the princes robed themselves in most beautiful sable vestments, and sat on the ground beside the cinders . . . throughout the night, extinguishing all the fire that was round about the sanctuary; and there they gave and received judgement, if any of them accused any of committing transgression. And when they had given judgement, they wrote the judgements, when it was light, upon a golden tablet, and dedicated them together with their robes as memorials.[19]

Atlantis lived in peace and prosperity, enjoying and exploiting her empire ". . . for many generations; and the wealth they possessed was so immense that the like had never been seen before in any royal house nor will ever easily be seen again."[20]

In his dialogue, *Critias*, Plato repeats the words of the Egyptian priest who spoke to Solon about the lost city of Atlantis. The priest offered five physical clues to the location of the city on Atlantis:

1. it was on a large plain;
2. near the ocean;
3. midway along the continent's greatest length;
4. towards the islands; and
5. surrounded by mountains.

Using these five clues and the climatic facts deduced from the theory of earth crust displacement, we can narrow the search for the city. (See Maps 25a to 25d.)

Map 25a shows that area of Antarctica outside the Antarctic Circle when Atlantis thrived. More than half of the island continent was under ice at that time. The city would not be found here. Thus the search can be restricted to Lesser Antarctica.

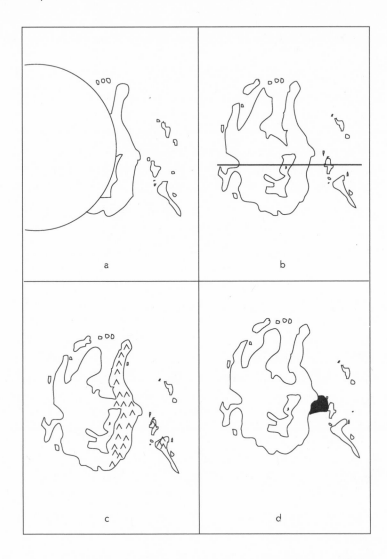

a

b

c

d

Maps 25a to 25d: The plain upon which the capital city stood will be found in a relatively small area of Antarctica once we view the continent without its ice. Clues to the location of the city of Atlantis are dictated by geology and detailed by Plato.

a. Hapgood's theory of earth crust displacement points to Lesser Antarctica because there was ice on Greater Antarctica during the reign of Atlantis.
b. The Egyptian priest tells us that the city of Atlantis was at the midpoint of the main island, towards the other islands.
c. The city was surrounded by mountains.
d. This area is the probable location of the lost city of Atlantis.

Plato tells us that the city was near the ocean, midway along the continent's greatest length and opposite the islands of Atlantis (Map 25b). It was completely surrounded by mountains and sat on a large plain on a small hill. The Antarctic mountain range runs along the coast on the same side as the small islands (Map 25c). The plain upon which the great city once probably stood is shown in Map 25d.

Such were the physical attributes of Atlantis according to the learned Egyptian priest. But its culture and civilization remain an intriguing mystery. Though a few tantalizing details are revealed by Plato, it remains the task of modern archaeology to excavate life from the cold grave of the lost city. It is to the icy, dark waters of Antarctica that we look to find answers about the very roots of civilization itself, answers that may yet be preserved in the frozen depths of the forgotten island continent.

But we need not fight the blizzards of Antarctica or burrow beneath its ice to view physical evidence of the Atlanteans' Golden Age. They left us a rich legacy of maps — saved by those lucky enough to escape the death of a continent. The ancient contours of the earth were copied, and recopied again and again, until eventually they fell into the hands of European explorers. The influence of these maps represent a lost chapter in the history of mixed blessings known as the "age of exploration." For before those rough, brave explorers set sail across the intimidating ocean, first they studied Atlantean maps.

Chapter Eight Atlantean Maps

In the winter of 332–331 B.C., Alexander the Great, then only twenty-four, led an army of thirty-five thousand troops through the unrelenting heat of the Sinai Desert. For seven days the procession marched upon barren rock. The sound of tramping boots, the clamour of armour, and the snorting of sweat-stained horses were muffled by the vast emptiness and unforgiving heat. Finally, Alexander led his men out of the desert and into the oasis that was Egypt. He had come to conquer this land as he had so many others.

Egypt's ruler, having no troops to oppose him, quickly surrendered.

While his troops wallowed in wine and soothed their limbs in Egyptian baths, Alexander pondered his future. His old tutor, Aristotle, had impressed upon him the wealth of treasures and untold secrets that could be found in the land of the pyramids. His strategic sense told him that Egypt, with desert lying to the west, south, and east, could be an easily defended haven, given adequate equipment and troops.

It was settled. He would establish a great city in Egypt, to become the western capital of his new empire. It would be called "Alexandria."

Alexander eventually left Egypt to pursue and vanquish the Persian armies before marching across even more distant lands. Finally, on the Beas River in present-day India, his exhausted troops refused to press onward. They had conquered the known world for their leader. They had had enough. Alexander led them back to Babylon, his eastern capital. There, before his thirty-third birthday, he died, leaving an empire that stretched a distance equal to the breadth of the United States.

Ptolemy, Alexander's childhood friend, returned his body to Egypt. There, Ptolemy established a Greek dynasty that would not end until fourteen kings had ruled and the final queen, Cleopatra, committed suicide as the Romans seized her domain. Ptolemy wouldn't rest until he had built a great library and museum fit to store all the secrets and treasures of the lands Alexander had conquered. To this end a great effort was made to bring all knowledge together in one place — Alexandria.

Preparations for this ambitious task were not made lightly. A hunt through the ancient lands of the Near East was begun, a hunt for long-hidden tablets, mysterious and intriguing maps, the secrets of ancient science, and artifacts to be carried to the museum.

For centuries the great library in Alexandria was the centre of learning in the world, sought out by all those who wished to follow the maze of their intellect and curiosity. Drawn like iron to magnets, scholars descended on Alexandria to study the secrets of long-lost civilizations.

One of the earliest librarians, Eratosthenes (c. 275–c. 195 B.C.), must have browsed through some incredible works. The secrets of geography, ancient maps, and accounts of daring travel were all closely guarded within the library's walls. Eratosthenes' great interest in geography took him to the ancient city of Syene on the Nile. While there he calculated, within a relatively small degree of error, the true circumference of the Earth. This feat he accomplished two and a half centuries before the birth of Christ.

Euclid (fl. c. 300 B.C.), whose name has become synonymous with geometry, studied at the marvellous library. Archimedes (287–212 B.C.), the "Thomas Edison" of the ancient world, spent day after day cloistered inside, unravelling the secrets of the ancient scrolls of Egypt. After his death, any great inventor was dubbed the "new Archimedes." But this gifted man was not infallible. He denigrated one of humankind's most significant discoveries.

The fact that the Earth revolves around the sun is common knowledge in our age, but in ancient Alexandria, this idea was considered ridiculous and Archimedes dismissed with contempt the heliocentric theory of Aristarchos of Samos. Aristarchos (fl. c. 270 B.C.) had come to Alexandria to mine the treasures of the great library. He developed the revolutionary idea that the Earth was in motion around the sun: an idea that was not accepted for another nineteen hundred years. Perhaps Aristarchos's inspiration lay in the pages of the texts of Atlantean sciences that lined the shelves of the library.

After the fall of Rome (476 A.D.) and Alexandria (642 A.D.), Constantinople became the world's centre of ancient maps. Here they would lie for centuries gathering dust until an unexpected threat arose from the north.

●

The sound of oars slicing through the waters of the misty fjords of northern Europe was heard more and more frequently during the ninth, tenth, and eleventh centuries. The Scandinavians, feeling the tensions of too many people in too little space, launched an invasion that would sweep through Europe. Dragon-prowed ships, with red-bearded men at the helm, were spied off the shores of England and France, and as far south as Italy. These were the Vikings, and their exploits in the southwest would be matched with excursions to Iceland, Greenland, and North America.

The story of the Vikings' daring voyages into the North Atlantic and ruthless acts of piracy in western Europe has overshadowed an even more amazing chapter in their history. In the early part of the ninth century, the eastern Vikings, who became known as the "Varangians," established a base in a city southeast of present-day St. Petersburg, which they called "Norovgorod." From Norovgorod they followed the mighty Volga and Dnieper rivers to the Black Sea and eventually on to Constantinople.

Constantinople, jewel of the Byzantine Empire, city of gold and pageantry, its splendour so renowned that it was known simply as the "Big City." In 860 A.D. the Varangians sacked the outer city but failed to penetrate its inner sanctum. After a final attempt to capture it failed, an alliance was forged between the Varangians and the Byzantine Empire in 941. By the middle of the tenth century, the Varangians were serving in increasing numbers in Constantinople's

Imperial Navy and became the first adventurers to set eyes on the ancient maps that were once housed in Alexandria's great library.

Copies of these maps may have found their way back to the Scandinavian homeland. The western Vikings turned the plunder to great advantage. As this cartographic treasure chest was opened to them they made their first discovery of new lands beyond the Atlantic. Erik the Red (c. 1000 A.D.), the discoverer of Greenland, and his son Leif Eriksson, the first European to reach America, led the long line of explorers who understood the true value of the maps of old Constantinople.

While the West was suffering the blight of the Dark Ages and enduring the pillages of the Vikings, the Islamic world was thriving in a golden age of learning. Much of the success of this brilliant era can be attributed to the Islamic Caliph's vision of an empire stretching from Spain to India. Abu-l-Abbas Abd-Allah al-Ma'mun was the Caliph (ruler) of an Islamic Empire that stretched west from Baghdad across North Africa into the Iberian Peninsula, and east all the way to India. One night the Caliph had a dream in which an old man appeared:

> It was as though I was in front of him, filled with fear of him. Then I said, "Who are you?" He replied, "I am Aristotle." Then I was delighted with him and said, "Oh sage, may I ask you a question?" He said, "Ask it." Then I asked, "What is good?" He replied, "What is good in the mind." I said again, "Then what next?" He replied, "What is good in the law." I said, "Then what is next?" He replied, "What is good with the public." I said, "Then what more?" He answered, "More? There is no more."[1]

A century after the death of Caliph al-Ma'mun, an Islamic writer told of the effects of the dream:

> This dream was one of the most definite reasons for the output of books. Between al-Ma'mun and the Byzantine emperor there was correspondence, for al-Ma'mun had sought aid opposing him. Then he wrote to the Byzantine emperor asking his permission to obtain a selection of old scientific [manuscripts], stored in the Byzantine country.[2]

In 833, on al-Ma'mun's orders, a library known as the "House of Wisdom" was established. The library, located in Baghdad, became for the Arabs what Alexandria had been for the ancient Greeks. The teachings of the Greeks were revived, and the scholars not only copied works but also introduced advancements in mathematics, and the forerunner of chemistry, alchemy.

Many centuries later, in 1559, an Arabic map of the earth was discovered. The "Hadji Ahmed World Map" of 1559 (see Map 26a) outlines the continent of North America in full, including areas that would not be mapped by Europeans until two centuries later.[3] This depiction is remarkable because the technology to measure a continent the size of North America requires an accurate determination of latitudes and longitudes.

Prince Henry of Portugal (1394–1460), one of the truly great minds of the fifteenth century, is often credited with perfecting the determination of latitude: how far north or south of the equator any given place is located. His cartographers knew that the height of the North Star above the horizon gives a close approximation of latitude. If the North Star is at a 50 degree altitude from the horizon, then the

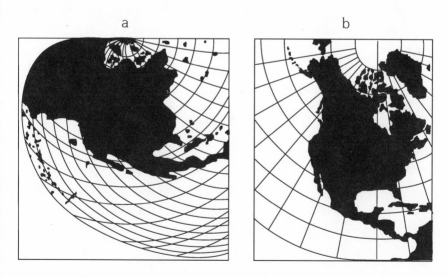

a b

Maps 26a & 26b: In 1559, long before it was explored by Europeans, the Hadji Ahmed World Map depicted a remarkably accurate North America. It may have originally been drawn by Atlanteans.

observer is near the fiftieth degree latitude. In the southern hemisphere, where there is no "South Star" by which to measure, the ship's captain would "shoot the sun" at noon each day to check for latitude. Astronomy was the answer to determining latitude.

The determination of longitude (how far east or west of the Prime Meridian [Greenwich, England, at 0 degrees]) was a much more complicated affair. The earth is a sphere that is divided into 360 degrees. Because it takes twenty-four hours to complete one revolution, one hour's "movement" of the sun equals 15 degrees (360 divided by 24). If it is noon at one spot on the earth, it is eleven o'clock 15 degrees to the west and one o'clock 15 degrees to the east. This means that to determine when it is noon where we are standing we must compare its time difference to Greenwich time.

Today we have radio and satellites to communicate with any spot on earth, but in the seventeenth century it wasn't possible to know the exact time at home if you were on the high seas.

The problem began to have serious ramifications in 1691 when seven British warships, lost because they couldn't measure their longitude, were shipwrecked off Plymouth. In 1694, a British fleet ran aground on Gibraltar for the same reason, and in 1707, two hundred lives and four ships were lost off the Scilly Isles because the British Navy had no way of determining longitude.

In 1714 the British Parliament set up the British Board of Longitude, which offered "a Publick Reward for such a Person or Persons as shall discover the Longitude at Sea." The prize was ten thousand pounds for the invention of a device that could determine a ship's longitude within one degree of an arc. The prize was upped to twenty thousand pounds if accuracy could be determined within half a degree. The device would be required to pass a test during a voyage to the West Indies (Caribbean). Twenty thousand pounds was a huge incentive in 1714, even for such a daunting task. In today's currency it would be worth nearly two million dollars.

In 1735, John Harrison (1693–1776) designed the first marine chronometer, a highly accurate clock.

In 1737, Harrison's marine chronometer was tested on a voyage to Lisbon and found to be accurate. The test trip to the West Indies had still to be sailed. Harrison's fourth, improved marine chronometer was tested on a trip to Jamaica in 1762 and passed easily. The Board of Longitude, in the tradition of all self-respecting bureaucracies, ensured the perpetuation of its own existence by refusing to grant the money to Harrison. He was given a partial payment of five thousand pounds in 1763 but not until King George III intervened on his behalf did the clever inventor receive the bulk of his reward in 1773. He was eighty years old.

Captain Cook made good use of the chronometer during his voyages to the South Seas in the 1770s. The device was checked for accuracy at the Greenwich Royal Observatory before his fleet cast off anchor. No matter where they were, the chronometer would tell exact Greenwich time. All Captain Cook had to do was determine noon, on any given day, and calculate the time difference to that at Greenwich. The difference in time could then be translated into degrees, west or east of Greenwich, to determine longitude. Armed with this new tool, the Europeans could, for the first time, map the shape of continents.

But the fact remains that some maps already showed the true contours of the continents. As mentioned above, the 1559 Hadji Ahmed map (Map 26a) shows the general shape, size, and position of North America, including what had been assumed to be the unexplored northwestern coast.

How could such a map exist when the technology required to construct it wasn't available in 1559? Perhaps the Atlanteans drew the source map for the Hadji Ahmed depiction? And for the people of Atlantis, North America was the least desirable continent. To them it was an unremarkable frozen land, much as Antarctica is regarded today. This map of North America depicts its shape not as it is in the present but as it was in the Atlanteans' time.

The discovery of radiocarbon dating since the Second World War enabled us to understand what North America looked like at 9600 B.C. When we superimpose the 1559 map of the continent over a modern archaeological map of the world of 9600 B.C., we see that the ancient map closely depicts what would correspond to an Atlantean view of North America (see Map 27).

If we could show a modern world map to a sailor of the Atlantean fleet he would be amazed. He would consider Antarctica to be drawn

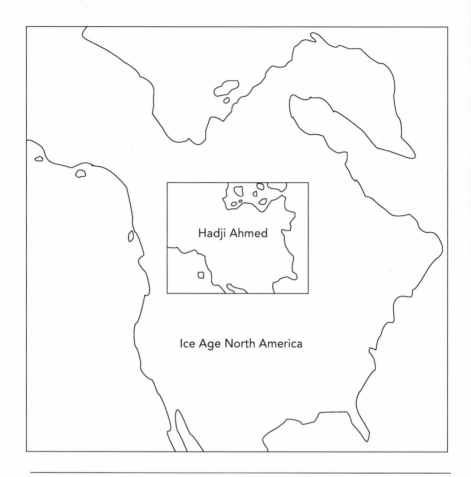

Map 27: When the Hadji Ahmed map of North America is compared to an estimate of the ice-covered shape of the continent as it was 11,600 years ago, the similarities are pronounced.

very inaccurately. Its bays, crevices, and archipelago are all hidden on our "modern" globe. He would question why the ocean covered so much more land. Why was it separated from the rest of the world at the place labelled "Alaska"? On the other hand, the sailor would immediately recognize the Hadji Ahmed map of North America as an accurate map of what he would consider a rather dull part of the world.

The existence of the ancient sub-continent of Beringia was not confirmed until the middle of the twentieth century. But here we find it depicted on the Hadji Ahmed map. It appears that the Arabs had gained possession of an Atlantean map of North America, drawn when most of it lay frigid beneath polar ice. And it would prove not to be the only map of Antarctica without its ice.

Those parched, well-worn maps were passed from hand to hand over generations, sometimes placed reverently in safekeeping by the wise men of the day, sometimes torn and crushed by the destructive tide of war. Until finally, they began to surface once again just as the "age of exploration" began.

●

On January 13, 812 A.D., Venice passed from the control of the Frankish Empire of Charlemagne to the Byzantine Empire and began an ascendancy that would continue for more than a millenium. Forged from a scattering of seafarers culled from the time of Attila the Hun (fifth century A.D.) to the city's entrance into the illustrious and wealthy Byzantine Empire, Venice was ideally situated on the Adriatic Sea. This proved to be the perfect location to profit from the expanding trade flow, as Europeans began to develop a taste for the exotic spices and an eye for the vibrant silks of Asia. Venice would come to dominate that trade for almost four centuries until the end of the twelfth, when the Byzantines began to see the advantage of trade with other cities such as Pisa and Genoa. The loss of this rich market provoked the Venetians. One man in particular, Enrico Dandolo, avenged the loss in a series of operations that led to the first successful attack on the fabulous city of Constantinople.

In 1198, a new pope was elected in Rome. Pope Innocent III was obsessed with the idea of a reunion of the Roman Catholic and Greek Orthodox Church. He hoped to accomplish this through the "Fourth Crusade," whose aim was to "liberate" Egypt and Palestine from the Islamic Empire and restore the Holy Land to a united Christianity. To fulfil this ambition he sent letters to all of Europe's kings requesting men and arms. Eventually a contingent of Crusaders arrived in Venice where they came under the command of Enrico Dandolo, the "Doge" (chief magistrate) of Venice.

Dandolo was a man consumed by a burning hatred of the Byzantines. His bitterness had been forged by a much more personal vendetta than a loss of trade. Dandolo had nursed his wrath for many years. Thirty years before, he had been taken hostage and: ". . . during his stay in Constantinople as a hostage, had been treacherously blinded by the Greeks by means of a concave mirror which strongly reflected the rays of the sun . . ."[4]

In the *History of the Byzantine Empire*: 324–1453, A.A. Vasiliev summarized the conditions that led to the attack upon Constantinople:

> Thus, in the preparations for the Fourth Crusade, two men were of first importance: Pope Innocent III, as a representative of the spiritual element in the crusade sincerely wished to take the Holy Land from the hands of the Muhammedans and was absorbed in the idea of union: and the Doge Enrico Dandolo, as a representative of the secular, earthly element, put first material, commercial purposes.[5]

Once Dandolo had command of the Crusade, he shifted the focus of the campaign until it eventually had nothing whatsoever to do with the Holy Land. First he unleashed the warriors onto the city of Zara, which had recently seceded from the Venetians. Here was a war of Christian versus Christian, a gross pillage, called a "Crusade." This "False Crusade" then turned towards the ultimate prize: Constantinople.

In June of 1203, the "Crusaders'" fleet arrived. A French soldier described the effect the great city had upon Dandolo's troops:

> Now you may imagine that those who had never before seen Constantinople looked upon it very earnestly, for they never thought there could be in all the world so rich a city, when they saw the high walls and magnificent towers that enclosed it round about, the rich palaces and mighty churches, of which there were so many that no one would have believed it who had not seen it with his own eyes — and the height and length of that city which above all others was sovereign. And be it known to you that no man was of such sturdy courage but his flesh trembled; and it was no wonder, for never was so great an enterprise undertaken by anyone since the creation of the world.[6]

On April 13, 1204, Constantinople fell. Vasiliev describes the scene:

> After taking the city, for three days, the Latins treated the city with appalling cruelty and pillaged everything which had been collected in Constantinople for many centuries. Neither churches, nor relics, nor monuments of art, nor private possessions were spared or respected . . . many libraries were plundered: manuscripts were destroyed.[7]

Dandolo had his revenge.

Maps, manuscripts, marble statues, and four life-size Alexandrian bronze horses were taken as the spoils of war to Venice. But another treasure, of a different sort, would arrive shortly before the end of the century.

In the late 1290s Marco Polo, his father, and his uncle arrived home in Venice after having spent more than two decades living in the heart of the Mongolian Empire of Kubilai Khan. Marco had been fifteen when he left Venice and he, his father, and uncle were unrecognizable to their own families after the long absence. The travellers arranged a great banquet to celebrate their homecoming. The event provided plenty of gossip as Marco's earliest biographer, John Baptist Ramusio, recorded:

> They invited a number of their kindred to an entertainment, which they took care to have prepared with great state and splendour in that house of theirs; and when the hour arrived for sitting down to the table they came forth of their chamber all three clothed in crimson satin, fashioned in long robes reaching down to the ground such as people in those days wore within doors. And when water for the hands had been served, and the guests were set, they took off those robes and put on others of crimson damask, whilst the first were by their orders cut up and divided among the servants. Then after partaking of some of the dishes they went out again and came back in robes of crimson velvet, and when they had again taken their seats, the second suits were divided as before. When

dinner was over they did the like with the robes of velvet, after they had put on dresses of the ordinary fashion worn by the rest of the company. These proceedings caused much wonder and amazement among the guests. But when the cloth had been drawn, and all the servants had been ordered to retire from the dining hall, Messer Marco, as the youngest of the three, rose from the table, and, going into another chamber, brought forth the three shabby dresses of coarse stuff which they had worn when they first arrived. Straightaway they took sharp knives and began to rip up some of the seams and welts, and to take out of them jewels of the greatest value in vast quantities, such as rubies, sapphires, carbuncles, diamonds and emeralds, which had all been stitched up in those dresses in so artful a fashion that nobody could have suspected the fact. For when they took leave of the Great Khan they had changed all the wealth that he had bestowed upon them into this mass of rubies, emeralds, and other jewels, being well aware of the impossibility of carrying with them so great an amount in gold over a journey of such extreme length and difficulty. Now this exhibition of such a huge treasure of jewels and precious stones, all tumbled out upon the table, threw the guests into fresh amazement, insomuch that they seemed quite bewildered and dumbfounded. And now they recognized that in spite of all former doubts these were in truth those honoured and worthy gentlemen of the Ca'Polo that they claimed to be; and as all paid them the greatest honour and reverence.[8]

Shortly after this marvellous occasion the young Polo became involved in one of the many wars that the Italian cities waged among each other. Unfortunately for him, but fortunately for literature and history, Marco Polo found himself a shackled prisoner of war in Genoa. He shared his cell with Rustichello of Pisa, a writer who also had had his freedom sacrificed to war. As they shuffled around the dark prison, Marco reminisced endlessly about his wondrous adventures in the East where he had been free in body and mind to explore the mysteries of an ancient civilization so strange and incomparable to his own.

The writer in Rustichello was awakened and fascinated. He urged Marco to allow him to record the adventures for posterity. Excitedly, he scribbled page after page and created a book that would fire the imagination of generations who grew thirsty for the treasures of the Orient, spurred on by the glimpses provided by the tales of Marco Polo.

Amidst the passion that gripped the Europeans for the silk, spices, gold, and precious stones of the East, a gem of a different sort was inadvertently passed over. Marco Polo had brought back, safely tucked within his precious jewels, a map of the world that showed the existence of a great southern island continent. The map depicts two circles inside a vast ocean. The top circle represents the world of Asia, Europe, and Africa. But it also reveals a southern counterpart. The notion of another continent located in the far south became, once again, a part of European geographic knowledge.

The idea of a great island continent in the southern hemisphere had drifted in and out of favour for many centuries. Pythagoras spoke of it in the sixth century B.C. and his tutor, Sonchis, described it in detail to Solon. But during the Dark Ages, knowledge of the island was lost to western Europe. After the fall of Rome, the use of Greek began to decline in the West and consequently only ancient books written in Latin were consulted.

The only work in Latin on ancient geography was written by Mela (fl. c. 43 A.D.) the famous Roman geographer. He taught that a climatic belt called the "Torrid Zone"[9] encircled the globe, dividing and separating the northern inhabitable regions from those in the south. He claimed that the Torrid Zone was so hot that the sea boiled there, and anyone who attempted to cross from one hemisphere to the other would be swallowed by the scalding waters. These teachings were fully accepted by most Christian priests of the Middle Ages.

However, it seemed to some that the existence of lands in the south, totally inaccessible because of the impassable Torrid Zone, raised serious questions of faith — questions concerning the salvation of the people whom Mela claimed lived on the other side of this great boiling barrier. If the word of Jesus could not be transmitted to these poor souls, how would they receive salvation? To answer this complex theological problem the priests came up with a simple solution: they burned all maps depicting any southern land. How many maps of Atlantis were destroyed we can never know. We do know that by the time Marco Polo had returned from the Orient with his treasured map, the existence of the great island continent in the south had been "forgotten."

The man who first took the terrible risk of exploring this "boiling" ocean was a Portuguese sailor by the name of Gil Eannes. Eannes took the chance, but the inspiration, funding, and will behind the effort originated with Prince Henry of Portugal.

The son of King John I and Queen Philippa, Henry had older brothers and so escaped most royal duties. This enabled the prince to pursue his passion for knowledge and discovery. Later generations called him "Prince Henry the Navigator," and his name ranks first and foremost in the annals of the modern scientific exploration of the globe.

At Sagres, on the Portuguese coast, Henry created a refuge for scholars. Here he voraciously collected all the maps, globes, and accounts of exploration that could be bought. In 1428, his older brother Pedro had been greeted with great respect when he travelled to Venice. He returned with two precious gifts for Henry. The first was a copy of the account of Marco Polo's travels. Henry was delighted with the book but even more thrilled by the second gift: a collection of world maps.[10]

It seems probable that some of these maps were once housed in the sacred cartography rooms of Constantinople and before that the library at Alexandria. These outlines of distant lands sketched across crumbling parchments became Henry's obsession. In his mind the maps were more than lifeless lines drawn by people long dead. He had to know where they led.

The problem wasn't simple. There were plenty of maps on offer that were the work of charlatans more than willing to sell "secrets" to the young prince. To address discrepancies between the various maps, Henry gathered together as many scholars as he could afford, and sometimes more than he could afford.

Finally, he concluded that the mystery could only be solved by launching a voyage into the void. He began preparations to equip vessels and crew for a vast project of exploration.

Convinced that the Torrid Zone was not impassable and therefore navigation of a southern route to India was possible, Henry instructed his captain, Eannes, to set sail for the south. The crew didn't share Henry's confidence in his secret maps. As the climate turned hotter and hotter they were convinced that it was only a matter of time before the very seas would be boiling. They kept turning back, pleading that the voyage was doomed. Henry decided he must speak to the sailors himself. He told them they would have to sail farther than ever before but that their fears were unfounded. Tales of boiling waters were fabrications. He appealed to their pride of seamanship and, more pragmatically, interest in material reward:

> If there were any authority for them, I could find an excuse for you. But indeed the stories are spread by men of little repute: the type of seamen who know only the coast of Flanders and how to enter well-known ports, and are too ignorant to navigate by compass and chart. Go forth, then, and heed none of their words; but make your journey straightaway. For the grace of God you can gain from this voyage nothing but profit and honour.[11]

The sailors were inspired and Captain Gil Eannes's voyage to the south dispelled once and for all the notion of an impassable Torrid Zone. A vast door swung open. The world seemed to shrink.

In 1432, Henry sent Goncalo Velho into the western sea to claim the islands that his maps revealed were there. Velho returned without sighting the Azores and insisted that they didn't exist. The Prince ordered the reluctant Velho to retrace his steps: "There is an island there, go back and find it."[12]

Henry's persistence paid off. The Azores were found and the doorway to the West as well as the South was open.

In 1453, Constantinople fell to the Turks and the last scholars fled

West. Their arrival in Italy is now considered one of the important causes of the Italian Renaissance. Others heard with relief that a Prince of Portugal would welcome scholars. Intellectual refugees poured into the city of Sagres, and Henry was overwhelmed with plans for potential discoveries. Because of Henry the Navigator's influence, Portugal became the new world centre for ancient maps.

In later centuries, several researchers, including Charles H. Hapgood, claimed that the Portuguese had early knowledge of undiscovered sections of America[13] and Antarctica.[14] It seems that they held accurate maps of undiscovered lands long before Columbus and the rest of the famous explorers set sail. Through a long, treacherous route carved by persecution and barbarism, Atlantean maps had fallen into Henry's hands. He not only saw their value and significance, but was also in a privileged position to act upon them.

Sixteen years after Henry's death, a young Italian adventurer was shipwrecked off the coast of Portugal. Having been wounded in a sea battle, Christopher Columbus clung desperately to broken fragments of his ship and swam for ten kilometres until he was washed upon the Portuguese shore. It was 1476, and he was welcomed and nursed back to health by a colony of Italian countrymen from his home city of Genoa. Columbus began a new career in the service of Portugal and settled down in Lisbon to become a mapmaker with his younger brother, Bartholomew. Eventually Christopher married into one of the most respected families of Portugal. His star began to rise.

Columbus's father-in-law had been a close friend of the now dead Prince Henry, and his mother-in-law was said to have given Christopher some greatly valued maps that her husband had left upon his death.[15] Nowhere on earth could the young Columbus have been better situated to begin his famous voyage westward. What secret maps he beheld and how many we don't know. But despite this great advantage he never achieved his quest to find a westerly route to India.

The man who did discover the route, and who proved the stunning fact that the world was round, was a Portuguese seaman who, like Columbus, sailed in the service of Spain after having learned his trade in Lisbon. Ferdinand Magellan was born of a noble Portuguese family in 1480. Magellan became a page to the Queen of Portugal and was required, as part of his education, to study all the arts of sailing, including cartography. In 1496, he became a clerical worker in the King of Portugal's marine department. He, even more than Columbus, had access to Prince Henry's wonderful collection of secret Atlantean maps.

Before he left for Spain, Magellan gained entry to the royal chartroom. There he found a globe that showed a strait at the tip of the still *unexplored* edge of South America. When he arrived at the Spanish court, Magellan proposed his plan to sail to India via a westerly route. A witness recorded his pitch to the royals: "Magellan had a well-painted globe in which the whole world was depicted, and on it he indicated the route he proposed to take, saving that the strait was left purposely blank so that no one should anticipate him."[16]

He set sail in 1519 with five ships. Crossing the Atlantic he followed the coast of South America to "discover" the straits that now bear his name. He named the Pacific Ocean but did not complete his journey around the globe. He was killed by natives in the Philippines. In 1522, one of his ships made a triumphant return to Spain, the first ship since the fall of Atlantis to have circumnavigated the globe.

In 1929, the year before its name was changed to Istanbul, the city of Constantinople yielded up one final jewel. An ancient map, dated 1513 and known as the Piri Re'is (after a Turkish admiral), was discovered in the old Imperial Palace.

The map eventually fell into the hands of an American, Captain Arlington H. Mallery. Mallery became convinced, after careful and minute studies of its details, that the southern section depicted an accurate outline of land that now lies buried beneath the Antarctic ice cap. This idea astounded Charles Hapgood, who was completing his work on the theory of earth crust displacement. Fascinated, in 1956, Hapgood began an extensive ten-year investigation (helped by his students at Keene State College) into the whole enigma of ancient maps.

One of Hapgood's students introduced him to the Chief of the Cartographic Section of Westover Air Force Base in Massachusetts.

After studying the map, Captain Lorenzo W. Burroughs concluded that the Antarctic portions did accurately depict the Princess Martha Coast of Antarctica and the Palmer Peninsula. That is, a map that first appeared in 1513 showed sections of Antarctica currently hidden under ice. The existence of these sections weren't recognized in modern times until 1949.

Lt. Colonel Harold Z. Ohlmeyer of the 8th Reconnaissance Technical Squadron wrote to Hapgood on July 6, 1960:

> The geographical detail shown in the lower part of the map agrees very remarkably with the results of the seismic profile made across the top of the ice cap by the Swedish-British-Norwegian Antarctic Expedition of 1949. This indicates the coastline had been mapped before it was covered by the ice cap. The ice cap in this region is now about a mile thick. We have no idea how the data on this map can be reconciled with the supposed state of geographic knowledge in 1513.[17]

(See Map 28.)

Hapgood and his students delved deeper into the mysterious world of ancient cartography. The Piri Re'is map yielded several more gems. It was found that parts of the Amazon River were depicted accurately long before that region of South America had been fully explored. But perhaps the most incredible thing about the map was that it had been drawn using an extremely sophisticated projection — an "equidistance projection" that depicts the features of the earth from one point on its surface. This point can centre on any spot on the earth's globe. Perhaps the most familiar equidistance projection is the blue and white flag of the United Nations, centred on the North Pole. To draw a map using this method requires a knowledge of advanced mathematics and instrumentation. A knowledge unrealized by the Europeans of 1513.

Hapgood and his students found to their astonishment that the original centre of the Piri Re'is map lay very close to the ancient Egyptian city of Syene on the Nile. (It was from there that Alexandria's librarian, Eratosthenes, had calculated the circumference of the Earth with remarkable accuracy.)

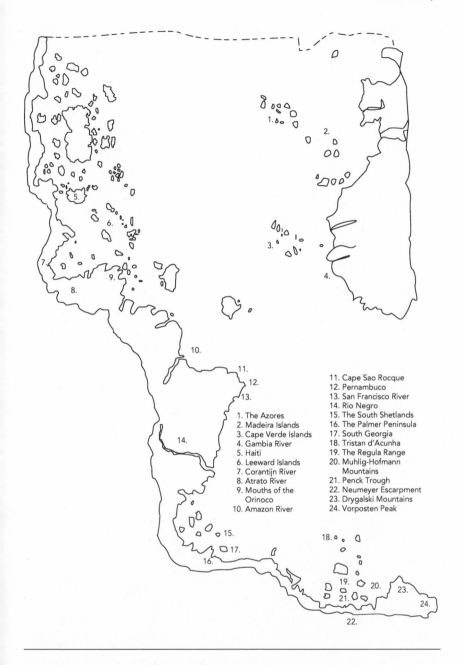

1. The Azores
2. Madeira Islands
3. Cape Verde Islands
4. Gambia River
5. Haiti
6. Leeward Islands
7. Corantijn River
8. Atrato River
9. Mouths of the Orinoco
10. Amazon River
11. Cape Sao Rocque
12. Pernambuco
13. San Francisco River
14. Rio Negro
15. The South Shetlands
16. The Palmer Peninsula
17. South Georgia
18. Tristan d'Acunha
19. The Regula Range
20. Muhlig-Hofmann Mountains
21. Penck Trough
22. Neumeyer Escarpment
23. Drygalski Mountains
24. Vorposten Peak

Map 28: In his book, *Maps of the Ancient Sea Kings*, Charles H. Hapgood revealed that the 1513 Piri Re'is map exhibited a knowledge of the true ice-free portions of Antarctica. The longitudes for twenty-four sites are accurate within one half a degree of the true positions. This standard of accuracy could not be matched until 1735 when John Harrison invented the marine chronometer.

After studying the ancient charts for ten years, Hapgood concluded in the preface to his new book, *Maps of the Ancient Sea Kings: Evidence of Advanced Civilization in the Ice Age*:

> This book contains the story of the discovery of the first hard evidence that advanced peoples preceded all the peoples now known to history. In one field, ancient sea charts, it appears that accurate information has been passed down from people to people . . . We have evidence that they were collected and studied in the great library of Alexandria and that compilations of them were made by the geographers who worked there. Before the catastrophe of the destruction of the great library many of the maps must have been transferred to other centers, chiefly, perhaps, to Constantinople, which remained a center of learning through the Middle Ages . . . It becomes clear that the ancient voyagers traveled from pole to pole. Unbelievable as it may appear, the evidence nevertheless indicates that some ancient people explored the coasts of Antarctica when its coasts were free of ice.[18]

In 1976 the authors came across another Atlantean map. It had been originally discovered by a meticulous researcher, Athanasius Kircher (1601–80), who claimed that it was an accurate Egyptian map of the lost continent of Atlantis. It had been stolen by the Romans during their occupation of Egypt and rediscovered in the seventeenth century by Kircher, a German Jesuit priest.

He was born to Anna Gansek and Johannes Kircher, a bailiff of the Abbey of Fulda in Germany. Johannes was very concerned about the fate of his sixth son who, it seemed, wouldn't amount to much. Athanasius was lazy and showed no special talent, except for getting into trouble. His first application to join the Society of Jesus, the Jesuits, was refused on the grounds of "insufficient mental ability." But a series of near fatal accidents brought focus to the boy's life.

> One was the near escape from drowning when Athanasius, while swimming in a forbidden pool, was swept down a

mill-race and under a mill wheel; another time it was an almost miraculous escape from being trampled to death, when, having worked his way to the front of a great crowd of onlookers, he was pushed out into the path of racing horses; finally there was the severe accident, resulting in a hernia, which came from an abortive attempt to show his skill in ice skating.[19]

His father impressed upon the boy his great fortune in surviving so many near misses, and finally, the man who would come to be known as the "universal genius" settled down to serious study. Eventually, in 1618, he was accepted by the Jesuits. The Order demanded physical fitness. Athanasius was afraid that his skating injury would jeopardize his position and tried to keep it secret. His limp, however, was noticed by the Fathers:

> . . . the ills from which I was suffering forced me to walk with tottering steps. My superiors immediately noticed this, and I was obliged to tell the whole story. A surgeon was called in. He was horrified at the state of my legs . . . and pronounced me incurable . . . I was told that since no medical attention could do me any good, I would be sent home from the Novitiate if I did not get better within a month.[20]

For the first time in his life, Kircher prayed for a miracle.

Within a few days he could walk with a steady gait. His place within the Order was secured.

The Jesuit scientists were amongst the most educated men in Europe, and Kircher's admission to their ranks ensured him as fine an education as was possible in the seventeenth century. Eventually he would rise "to hold the most honourable place among these scientists of the Society of Jesus."[21] But the road would be a long one. He was showing great promise when the Thirty Years War erupted over Germany. Kircher and his fellow Jesuits were forced to flee the invading armies in the dead of winter with insufficient clothing and no food. His biographer, Conor Reilly, wrote:

> He would never forget the sufferings of that journey. Snow was deep on the roads, and in the war-devastated

countryside the young Jesuits could find little food or shelter. Exhausted and hungry they finally reached the Rhine. The river was frozen over. On the advice of the local people, who took them for deserters from one of the warring armies, they began to cross the ice. It seemed quite solid but Kircher, who was leading the way, suddenly saw open water before him. He turned back, but a gap had opened between him and his companions; he was trapped on an island of ice. The river current caught the floe on which he stood and swung it out into midstream. His companions could do nothing to help: they implored God and His Blessed Mother to save him; they watched as he was swept along, until he was out of sight; then they crossed the river at another point and made their way to a Jesuit College on the west bank of the Rhine.

Hours later, stiff and blue and bruised and bleeding, Kircher struggled up to the door of the college. To the joy of his companions, who had been praying for the repose of his soul, he told how his ice-floe had been jammed among others down stream, permitting him to clamber along towards the further shore. He had had to swim a wide gap before he finally reached dry land.[22]

Kircher's legend was already being forged. He resumed his studies with even greater enthusiasm. Astronomy fascinated him and through the concentrated use of a telescope he announced the rather startling idea, at the time, that the sun was made of the same material as the earth. He was the first to propose that the sun was an evolving star.

In 1628 Kircher was ordained as a priest. Soon a new interest began to draw his attention — archaeology. One day, while browsing in a Jesuit library, he came upon illustrations of Egyptian obelisks. The hieroglyphic inscriptions fascinated him. Later, he was appointed by successive popes to study and restore the obelisks. Egypt's intimate connection with the Bible made the deciphering of these figures of critical interest to the Church and they had chosen a man more than well-qualified for the task.

His other pursuits followed not only the explosive macro-worlds of astronomy and geology, but also the silent micro-world beneath the lens of a microscope. From these early explorations he introduced the then revolutionary idea that microbes were the cause of disease. A true Renaissance man, he sought knowledge wherever it led him. After an eruption of Mount Vesuvius, he went so far as to lower himself into the steaming crater to view its violent upheavals first-hand. He also taught physics, mathematics, and Oriental languages at the prestigious College of Rome. In 1643, Kircher resigned his post to devote himself fully to the study of his true love, archaeology.

By 1665 he had produced the first volume of his encyclopaedic work, *Mundus Subterraneus*. It was a massive book, brimming with ideas, illustrations, and the results of his intricate research into the mysteries of alchemy. In this book, Kircher claimed that the remains of Atlantis lay beneath the North Atlantic Ocean. He revealed the mysterious map of Atlantis that he claimed had been stolen from Egypt by the early Roman invaders. (See Map 29.)

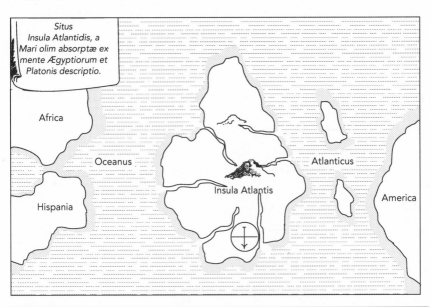

Map 29: In 1665, Athanasius Kircher published this Egyptian map of Atlantis showing north as "down." For generations, researchers have misguidedly turned this map upside down so that America appears on the left and Spain on the right. There is, however, an alternative depiction.

The inscription on the map translates: "Site of the island of Atlantis, now beneath the sea, according to the beliefs of the Egyptians and the description of Plato." At first glance, the map seems odd to modern eyes because north, as indicated by the downward pointing compass, is at the bottom of the page. But the ancient Egyptians believed that south lay in the direction of the headwaters of the sacred Nile. Therefore south must be "up." Kircher reproduced this belief.

The map appears much more familiar to us if we look at it upside down. America then appears on the left and Spain and North Africa on the right — where we are accustomed to seeing them in twentieth century maps.

If we lift a modern globe off its limiting hinges and roll it about like a beach ball so that the South Pole faces us, placing South America on our right and South Africa and Madagascar on our left, we can immediately see that the Egyptian map of Atlantis represents in size, shape, scale, and position, an ice-free Antarctica (see Map 30).

The present shape of Antarctica as depicted is based upon the current ocean level, not that of 11,600 years ago. Atlantis did not actually sink beneath the waves. Instead, as the old ice caps melted, the ocean level rose, covering some of the continent's permutations. Further distortions in our modern map, compared to Kircher's, are a result of the weight of today's Antarctic Ice Sheet. This immense blanket of snow and ice depressed parts of the continent, causing more and more land to fall below ocean level. Nevertheless, the shadow of Atlantis can still be seen in the modern map of Antarctica.

If the horror of an earth crust displacement were to be visited upon today's interdependent world culture, the progress of thousands of years of civilization would be torn away from our planet like a fine cobweb. Those who live near high mountains might escape the global tidal waves but they would be forced to leave behind, in the lowlands, the slowly constructed fruits of civilization. Only among the merchant marine and navies of the world might some evidence of civilization remain. The rusting hulls of ships and submarines would eventually perish but the valuable maps that are housed in them would be saved by survivors — perhaps for

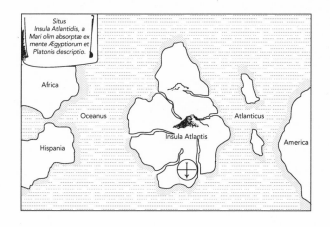

Map 30: If we compare Kircher's Egyptian map of Atlantis with a modern geophysical globe that shows the south as "up," our perspective changes. With this southern perspective the segments of the map that Kircher labelled "Hispania" (Spain) are actually seen as southern Africa. "Africa" becomes Madagascar, and South America is "America." Atlantis is shown to be Antarctica. Kircher's map was published almost three centuries before we knew the true ice-free shape of Antarctica.

hundreds, even thousands of years — until once again they could be used to sail the World Ocean and rediscover lost lands.

And perhaps the survivors might one day have the leisure and the will to pursue their lost past. Perhaps they would launch an expedition to the pole to unveil the ice-covered remains of a lost city.

Chapter Nine Mythology Unmasked

There has been a cycle in the quest for knowledge. We began in humility, appealing to the gods to protect us from the unknown. Later, we imagined a world perfectly ordered by God's divine will. But it was faith in reason that transformed us from believers in supernatural intervention into followers of the creed of progress. And now we have come full circle, once again humbled by the immensity of the universe. We no longer cast spells against the unknown; we cast spacecraft into the void.

The story of our search for order and pattern has been lost in the mute, unwritten past. For before science, there was magic. Magic was a tool of the hunter when he drew stark images of animals over fire-lit cave walls. Through magic the shaman hoped to secure the future, but a future that never dared to challenge the elder's myths. It was taboo to doubt the gods. This inhibition was the fatal flaw in the design woven by these early magicians. All was explained but little was truly understood. The power of magic was destined to flounder, for without the freedom to cast doubt upon an idea, there can be no genuine inquiry. And without inquiry, magic could not evolve into science.

The hunger to command and the need to pilot our fate have been among humankind's most persistent quests. Science has shone a great light along the shadowy road but it has been a bumpy ride. Unlike the shaman or priest, scientists must by the very nature of their calling be willing to tamper with taboos. From this struggle there emerged a new way of seeing the world, and a new way of learning and knowing.

For millennia, our world view was clouded by the mist of magic and myth. But then, quite suddenly, six centuries before the birth of Christ, came a clearing. On the eastern shore of the Mediterranean Sea, the Ionian Greeks burst forth with a fresh and energetic way of seeing the world. They heralded the death of magic and the birth of science.

The first "immortal" to be struck down by the new sword of science was the Olympian god of the sea: Poseidon. As master of the ocean he commanded the respect, awe, and honour of all seafaring Greeks. Poseidon was a violent god who carried within his arsenal the dreaded weapon of the earthquake. Since the land of the Greeks had often fallen victim to earthquakes, Poseidon was not only worshipped, but feared. It is not surprising then, given this fear, that the Greeks were disturbed when one of the seven wise men, Thales (c. 636–546 B.C.), suggested that the fearful rumbling of the earth was not controlled by the powerful Poseidon.

Thales may have acquired his materialistic explanation of the cause of earthquakes while visiting Egypt. We are told that ". . . he went to Egypt and spent some time with the priest there."[1] Thales set no bounds on his curiosity and delved into the enigmas of the soul as well as solutions to the mysteries of the universe. In some lines attributed to him we can touch the depth of his intellect:

> Of all things that are, the most ancient is God, for he is uncreated. The most beautiful is the universe, for it is God's workmanship. The greatest is space, for it holds all things. The swiftest is mind, for it speeds everywhere. The strongest, necessity for it masters all. The wisest, time, for it brings everything to light.[2]

But above all Thales dared to doubt. He argued that the island-earth was like a great ship at sea, which as it rocked upon the waters, caused earthquakes. Thales had proclaimed the unthinkable. He had usurped the role of a god by providing a physical explanation for a natural phenomenon. Thales thus became the world's first scientist. He began that long, relentless battle that even in our time is waged between faith and reason, myth and science.

It is accepted opinion today that mythology and science are like oil and water: they don't mix. But like Thales we should always be willing to cast doubt upon accepted opinion. If we use science as our torch, a pathway can be made through the darkness of mythology: myth and science need not always collide.

Thales found order within the universe: gods and goddesses were no longer needed to unravel the powers of nature. Human beings could do it alone. It would take centuries before this radical notion was to find its proper place in history. Until then another explanation for the mystery of the actions of the gods was needed.

In the fourth century B.C., a Sicilian by the name of Euhemerus wrote *Sacred History*, in which he argued that the exploits of the gods and goddesses of ancient times were simply exaggerated tales of the real deeds of former kings and queens. Thus was born the first school of mythology.

The idea was simple yet provocative. Myths were signposts to the past. They might be used to recapture the lost lines of history. They were disguised truths that might lead us to hidden treasures, lost cities, perhaps even lost continents. But this "lost history" school of mythology never became widely accepted. The people of Rome preferred to believe in the reality of their gods and goddesses. Christians sought paradise in the afterlife, not on earth. More recently, the lost history approach to mythology has been discredited by the writings of Erich von Daniken and Immanuel Velikovsky (1895–1979). These two writers used myths *as evidence* for events they believed occurred in the remote past. Such an approach is always open to wild speculation. Without roots in science the interpretation of myths is a risky business.

The first great mythologist of the modern age was the son of an Italian bookseller. Giambattista Vico (1668–1744) was a self-educated scholar who saw myths as valuable keys to understanding human culture and the workings of the mind. Each of these two approaches, cultural and psychological, evolved into separate schools of thought.

Vico believed that societies move through various stages of development and that each stage produced a corresponding level of mythology: ". . . the fables originating among the first savage and crude men were very severe, as befitted the founding nations emerging from a state of fierce bestial freedom."[3]

Myths in this anthropological approach are vital keys to understanding culture. Each culture is seen as a unique and self-contained unit. Vico recognized the limitations of this interpretation and augmented it by comparing myths from around the world. "Uniform ideas originating among entire peoples unknown to each other must have a common ground of truth."[4]

Unlike the lost history school, or the culturally specific approach, Vico offered the prospect of finding common ground in the nature of the human mind. "There must in the nature of human things be a mental language common to all nations, which uniformly grasps the substance of things . . ."[5]

This school of mythology found forceful proponents in the writings of the English anthropologist Sir Edward Burnett Tylor (1832–1917) and the psychiatrists Sigmund Freud (1856–1939) and Carl Jung (1875–1961). More recently the French anthropologist Claude Lévi-Strauss (1908–) and the American mythologist Joseph Campbell (1904–87) have enriched this approach to myths.

For Tylor the fascination lay within the commonality of myths from around the world:

> The treatment of similar myths from different regions, by arranging them in large compared groups, makes it possible to trace in mythology the operation of the imaginative processes recurring with the evident regularity of mental law; and thus stories of which a single instance would have been a mere isolated curiosity, take their place among well-marked and consistent structures of the human mind.[6]

Sigmund Freud believed that the mind filters memories to suit its present state and distrusted myths as an accurate representation of real events:

> One is thus forced by various considerations to suspect that in the so-called earliest childhood memories we

possess not the genuine memory-tree but a later revision of it, a revision which may have been subjected to the influences of a variety of later psychical forces. Thus the "childhood memories" of individuals come in general to acquire the significance of "screen memories" and in doing so offer a remarkable analogy with the childhood memories that a nation preserves in its store of legends and myths.[7]

Carl Jung took the idea of myths as doorways to the mind even further than Freud. Like Vico, Jung was fascinated by the appearance of similar myths around the globe:

Although traditional transmission by migration certainly plays a part there are, as we have said, very many cases that cannot be accounted for in this way and drive us to . . . assume the existence of a collective psychic substratum. I have called this the *collective unconscious*.[8]

Like Freud and Jung, Claude Lévi-Strauss seeks in myths the clues to the workings of the mind: ". . . the purpose of myth is to provide a logical model capable of overcoming a contradiction . . ."[9]

Joseph Campbell summarizes the contribution of this school of mythology:

The bold and truly epoch-making writings of the psycho-analysts are indispensable to the student of mythology; for, whatever may be thought of the detailed and some-times contradictory interpretations of specific cases and problems, Freud, Jung and their followers have demon-strated irrefutably that the logic, the heroes, and the deeds of myth survive into modern times. In the absence of an effective general mythology, each of us has his private, unrecognised, rudimentary, yet secretly potent pantheon of dream.[10]

For Campbell the myths provide pathways to ethical wisdom and offer beacons of spiritual guidance. In his view, to look at them as potential lost history is missing the spiritual dimension altogether.

From Vico to Campbell, mythologists have sought the key to the puzzle of the nature of imagination and thought. In this book we have examined many myths that speak of the lost island paradise and have explored the significance of the sun-deluge motif. But we do not offer the myths as concrete evidence, although we do believe that these ancient renditions represent something more than just evidence of the similarity of humanity's mental makeup.

We propose that certain myths do indeed represent lost history but this conjecture is based upon the capacity of the earth crust displacement theory to provide order to recognized, long-standing problems in science.

The noted sociologist of science Thomas S. Kuhn lists five key characteristics of a good scientific theory: ". . . accuracy, consistency, scope, simplicity and fruitfulness — are all standard criteria for evaluating the adequacy of a theory."[11]

The "simplicity" of the theory of earth crust displacement drew Albert Einstein to Hapgood's idea. Hapgood replaces the presupposition of a relatively stable crust with the notion that the crust shifts. Using this simple assumption, the theory is capable of accurately and consistently addressing a wide scope of established problems. It provides a framework with which to comprehend the mysterious myths of the lost island paradise and the worldwide appearance of the sun-deluge motif. And it offers an explanation of why some ancient maps are so strangely accurate — maps that appear to have originated in an unknown civilization. The theory also points to Lesser Antarctica as the site of Atlantis.

But what have others believed about the lost continent?

•

When Solon, the history of Atlantis still swirling in his head, returned to Athens from Egypt, Pythagoras (c. 582–c. 507 B.C.) was a young man on the Greek island of Samos. Pythagoras was drawn, like Solon, to seek out the whispered secrets he had heard about the past. This search lured him from the lush olive groves of Samos to journey to the banks of the fabled Nile. When Pythagoras at last met the learned priests of Sais he presented each with a large silver wine bottle. One of the priests, named Sonchis, became Pythagoras's tutor. Perhaps he was the same Sonchis who had shared the secret of Atlantis with Solon.

His tutors instilled the habit of secrecy well in Pythagoras. What he learned about the lost continent we cannot know for certain. All we do know of his teachings comes to us second-hand. But he was the first to claim that the earth was round and ". . . inhabited round about. There are also antipodes, and our 'down' is their 'up.'"[12]

Pythagoras was also the first to teach that five climatic zones belt the earth and that a southern continent did indeed exist. Six centuries after his death, Mela, the Roman geographer who gave Europe the notion of the impassable Torrid Zone, published a map of the world that included Pythagoras's southern island continent of "Antichthones." (See Map 31.)

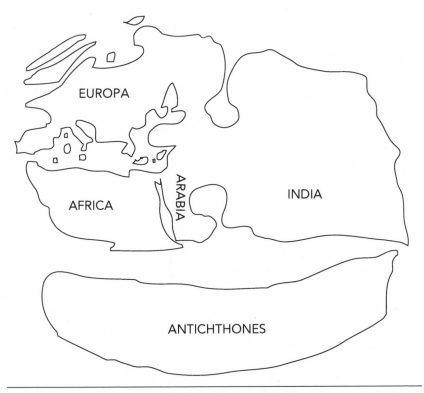

Map 31: The Roman geographer Mela adopted Pythagoras's idea of a great southern island continent called "Antichthones." Sonchis, the priest who told Solon about Atlantis, may have been the same priest who became tutor to Pythagoras. Did both Greeks receive parts of the great puzzle?

Pythagoras established a brotherhood in the Italian city of Croton. The community was eventually overthrown in a revolt that may have taken the teacher's life. The Roman poet Ovid (43 B.C. –A.D. 18) claimed to have the text of a speech the great philosopher gave to the citizens of Croton:

> For my part, considering how the generations of men have passed from the age of gold to that of iron, how often the fortunes of differing places have been reversed, I should believe that nothing lasts long under the same form. I have seen what once was solid earth now changed into sea, and lands created out of what was ocean . . . ancient anchors have been found on mountain tops.[13]

Like Sonchis, Pythagoras shared the belief that what is most ancient is most perfect. This attitude is hard for those of us who live in the late twentieth century to grasp. For unlike the children of ancient Greece and Egypt who were raised with myths that spoke of perfect beings who thrived in ancient times, children now gaze at incredible science fiction projections of the future. Although our confidence is sometimes shaken, it is still to the future, rather than the past, that we look for perfection.

The idea of "progress" has penetrated current thinking so completely that it is vaguely disturbing, yet endlessly fascinating, to learn of the great achievements of ancient Egypt, Mexico, or Peru. Impressive ruins shake our sense of the inevitable march of progress and make us wonder about our own future. That an advanced civilization thrived and then perished in remote times is an uncomfortable realization for those who believe in the inevitability of progress.

After Plato's death, his student Aristotle became the foremost philosopher in Athens. Aristotle was said to be highly skeptical about Homer's famous legend of Troy. "He who brought it into existence can also cause it to disappear . . ."[14]

These words were later used falsely in reference to Plato's account of Atlantis, giving rise to the idea that Atlantis was entirely the product of Plato's lively imagination. But as we have shown, the "story" of Atlantis, under different names, has been rewritten again and again in the myths of peoples with whom Plato could not possibly have had any contact. The Haida and Okanagan myths of a lost land and the Cherokee notion of a floating island in the southern hemisphere are not ideas that Plato could have borrowed. Nor was he likely to have been aware of the ancient Iran/Indian ice-covered island paradise of Airyana Vaêjo, nor Japan's Onogorojima. And Aztlan, the lost white island of the ancient people of Mexico, owes nothing to Plato.

Crantor (c. 300 B.C.) was one of the first to write extensively about Plato's dialogue *Timaeus*. He was strongly convinced of the truth of the account of Atlantis and went so far as to send envoys to Egypt to verify the story. When the messengers returned they confirmed that the legend was ". . . written on pillars which are still preserved."[15]

Crantor believed Atlantis was a real place that had existed in the North Atlantic Ocean. As time went by, this became the most popular location for the lost continent — an idea, as we have seen, based upon a misunderstanding of the term "Atlantic Ocean." The age of exploration opened up land to the west and intriguing possibilities for the situation of Atlantis. The vanished continent would surely be found in Central America, North America, or Brazil. As other lands were explored, it was South Africa, Ceylon, Greenland, and so on. Eventually, however, the North Atlantic Ocean re-emerged as the favourite site. Athanasius Kircher, the Jesuit who discovered the Egyptian map of Atlantis, was also convinced that it lay beneath the North Atlantic. His influence was great because he was widely believed to be the most learned man in the world. After his death (1680) the dialogue was reduced to a debate between those who thought, like Kircher, that Atlantis had sunk beneath the ocean and was thus lost forever, and those who held out hope that some yet undiscovered land would prove to be the lost paradise. All this changed in 1882 with Ignatius Donnelly's book *Atlantis: The Antediluvian World*.

Ignatius Donnelly (1831–1901) is one of the most colourful figures in the story of the search for Atlantis. Born in Philadelphia, he studied law before moving to Minnesota where he was elected Lieutenant-Governor at the age of twenty-eight. He was then elected to Congress and spent most of his time absorbed by the rich resources of the Library of Congress. Two topics consumed him. In his book *The Great Cryptogram* he presented the results of his analysis, which concluded that Sir Francis Bacon was the real author of Shakespeare's plays. But it was writing about Atlantis that made him one of the most popular lecturers in America. Like Kircher, Donnelly believed that Atlantis lay beneath the North Atlantic Ocean. He was excited by the idea that a marvellous new invention, the submarine, would transform the search into a reality.

His popular book boldly asserted that the description of Atlantis offered by Plato was not, as had long been supposed, a fable, but actual history. He believed that Atlantis:

> . . . became, in the course of ages, a populous and mighty nation, from whose overflowings the shores of the Gulf of Mexico, the Mississippi River, the Amazon, the Pacific coast of South America, the Mediterranean, the west coast of Europe and Africa, the Baltic, the Black Sea, and the Caspian were populated by civilized nations.[16]

The idea of Atlantean colonies was a popular one in a newly independent America. However, even if it were true, the remains of such colonies would have perished long ago. We barely have enough artifacts from the oldest known civilization, Sumeria, to piece together its history. Most of its remains have disintegrated into the dust of time. Any Atlantean colonies would be at least twice as old as Sumeria and highly unlikely to survive nearly twelve thousand years of weathering. Donnelly also surmised "that the oldest colony formed by the Atlanteans was probably in Egypt, whose civilization was a reproduction of that of the Atlantic island."[17] The newly discovered ancient age of the Great Sphinx as documented by John Anthony West and Dr. Robert Schoch gives new support to this claim.[18]

Donnelly's book sent America spinning into an Atlantean fever. In 1883, New Orleans devoted its Mardi Gras to the Atlantis theme.[19] Donnelly was elected to the American Association for the Advancement of Science. By 1890 the book had gone to press for twenty-three editions. It is still in print today.

Three years after the publication of Donnelly's work, the founder and president of Boston University, William Fairfield Warren (1833–1929) published his *Paradise Found: The Cradle of the Human Race at the North Pole*. This book used comparative mythology and the latest theories of geology to tackle the question of the lost paradise, of which Atlantis is but one story. His geological idea, as we have seen, did not survive, and consequently his whole investigation has been ignored despite the fact that it was much more comprehensive than Donnelly's. Because he believed that paradise was once at the North Pole Warren didn't restrict his investigation to lands on either side of the North Atlantic Ocean. He examined myths from all around the globe, finding a great deal of mythology that associated the lost paradise with the pole. He launched the research tradition that treated the lost land as a real place located in a remote region of the world that had been destroyed by a global catastrophe.

Unlike the "remote" school of thought, which derives its momentum from a geological theory of catastrophe coloured by comparative mythology, the most recent investigations of Atlantis take an entirely different line. The "regional" school of thought finds its strength in archaeological evidence of a vanquished civilization and geological support for a local catastrophe that destroyed it.

Although unaware of it, Charles Lyell, the great uniformitarian geologist, was the first scientist to lay down the arguments that would eventually form one of the backbones of the "regional" approach to the problem of Atlantis. In his *Principles of Geology* (first volume, 1830), Lyell was concerned with the worldwide stories of a great flood. His uniformitarian beliefs led him to belittle them:

> The true source of the system must be sought for in the exaggerated traditions of those partial, but often dreadful catastrophes, which are sometimes occasioned by various combinations of natural causes.[20]

This idea of exaggeration would come to play a central role in the "modern" thought about Atlantis. But the idea of a small, localized Atlantis was launched after Sir Arthur Evans (1851–1941) excavated the remains of the Minoan civilization on Crete. Nine years later, on February 19, 1909, an article appeared in the London *Times* under the title "The Lost Continent." It was written by a young man who was on the staff of Queen's University in Belfast. K. T. Frost argued that Evans's discovery meant Crete might have been Atlantis. Frost was killed in action in the First World War but his idea would be taken up on the threshold of the Second World War.

In 1939, Professor Spyridon Marinatos, Director of the Greek Archaeological Service, put forward the idea that a volcanic explosion had occurred on the island of Thera, just north of Crete. In the 1950s and 1960s, Professor Angles Galanopoulos dated the debris from the Thera eruption to 1500 B.C., a time corresponding with the fall of the Minoan civilization. Was Thera Atlantis?

The classical account of the Thera/Crete as Atlantis theory was written in 1969 by J.V. Luce, a classics and philosophy lecturer at Trinity College, Dublin, in his book *The End of Atlantis: New Light on an Old Legend*.[21] His theory disputes much of Plato's account. Luce treats the "story" as an exaggeration of the actual fall of Crete, which, in turn, was triggered by the volcanic explosion on Thera.

Luce's theory fails as an account of Atlantis. Plato's Egyptian priest describes Atlantis as being larger than Libya (North Africa) and Asia (the Middle East) combined. It is an island continent. Such an immense land could never be found within the confines of the Mediterranean Sea. Moreover, Plato's account directs our attention to Atlantis beyond the Pillars of Heracles (Strait of Gibraltar). Atlantis was said to be in the real ocean of which the Mediterranean Sea is but a small harbour. The Crete theory ignores the sun-deluge motif and distorts the timing of events by a factor of ten. It ignores the description of great mountains and high altitude.

While it may be true that a volcanic explosion on Thera destroyed Crete, there is no justification in tying it to the legend of Atlantis. The Crete theory of Atlantis conveniently treats Plato's account as unreliable, exaggerated, and garbled. But when Antarctica is substituted as a reference point, the same account becomes clear.

In 1979, Harald A.T. Reiche, a professor of classics and philosophy at M.I.T., published "The Language of Archaic Astronomy: A Clue to the Atlantis Myth?" in which he argues that the layout of the city of Atlantis mirrors "features of the southern circumpolar sky." In other words, the various rings of the city of Atlantis equate to the layout of the stars in the *southern* hemisphere. Reiche sees in Plato's account "an embellished version of what in original intention was a map of the sky."[22]

Again and again people return to Plato's famous account to squeeze yet another clue from it. Why have these attempts always failed? The original meanings of the Greek terms "Atlantic Ocean" and "Pillars of Heracles" have been consistently misunderstood. These mistakes, as we have seen, restricted the search for Atlantis to either the North Atlantic Ocean or the Mediterranean Sea. But Atlantis was in the "real ocean," the "World Ocean" of oceanographers. And it wasn't until the earth's violent history was known that we could look beyond the northern hemisphere for the lost land.

But the mystery isn't over — only transformed. Even more exciting questions lie ahead. How advanced were the Atlanteans? What did their art, science, and customs reveal of their hopes, dreams, and fears? These are the great mysteries that remain.

●

If we were to judge them by their engineering feats alone, the Atlanteans must have had advanced knowledge of the physical sciences. There are hints in the construction of the Great Sphinx[23] of Egypt and the Temple of the Sun on Lake Titicaca in South America that the Atlanteans could move stones weighing in excess of two hundred tons with apparent ease. One fallen obelisk in Ethiopia weighed more than five hundred tons.[24] And at Ramesseum, in Luxor, one shattered stone, representing Ramses the Great, once weighed more than one thousand tons when it was whole.[25] The science of moving great objects, such as those used in the temples of the Sphinx, is beyond the limits of today's fossil-fuel-driven cranes.[26]

If the ancient maps that Hapgood and his students examined in the 1960s are any indication, the Atlanteans had mapped the entire globe, something that we only completed in the twentieth century with our explorations of Greenland and Antarctica.

There is evidence that they created a language that can communicate flawlessly with computers and that may have served as a universal translator.[27] And all around the globe the sudden rise of early agricultural experiments date to the very century (9600 B.C.) during which the Egyptian priest says Atlantis fell.[28]

What we are dealing with is not just another lost ancient civiliza-tion, it is a lost *advanced* culture, one possessing scientific knowledge that we have yet to comprehend. Who knows what problems might be solved by the discovery of the lost sciences of Atlantis? And one can only wonder about the lost art, sculpture, and architecture lying beneath the ice. Whoever takes up the search should remember that the remains of Atlantis might cradle an unimaginable heritage.

But already the promise of treasure of another sort — minerals, fishing grounds, unique laboratory conditions — have led to polite grumbling around the negotiation table as claim and counterclaim to slices of the last continent are argued.

We surely must proceed with caution if we decide to disturb this pristine place. Behind the deceptively rigid white mask lies a conti-nent that is home to many forms of life bound in a delicate chain vulnerable to the brutal mechanics of technology.

It is ironic that beneath Antarctica — centre of one of our most dramatic environmental alarms, the depletion of the ozone layer — may lie the smothered evidence of the most overwhelming environ-mental disaster.

Beneath the splendour of the Southern Lights, human garbage al-ready scums the gleaming snow and the giant skeletal remains of machinery rusts against the horizon. Plastic containers float in the black sea and dynamite blasts rip through the eternal silence. This place offers great promise and a great opportunity — maybe a last chance for human beings to touch with some dignity, some sensitivity, the creatures that still live there. Perhaps this unique exploration, unlike many of the others we have seen in these pages, can be tempered with mercy. We might start by declaring Antarctica an international park, the responsibility of us all. We could use only the most sophisticated, least intrusive, instru-ments to peer beneath the ice. If evidence of civilization is found, a surgical probe could be made. We would hold our breath as we waited to glimpse the ancient city locked in ice.

The quest would be reborn.

Our past and future would meet.

Science and myth might merge.

Afterword

by John Anthony West

An afterword presupposes that readers have already read the book under discussion — apart from that minority of browsers who like to nibble fore and aft before biting into the bait.

If you have indeed read this book through, you may have come to the same conclusion I have: the evidence assembled by the Flem-Aths is compelling.

Anyone reading or researching deeply into the distant past soon comes up against glaring anomalies in the currently accepted scenario of pre-history. Deluge myths are universal around the world, and the mythologies of widely separated peoples tell, over and over again, variations of the same story of global cataclysm. Plato's infamous Atlantis legend, in all its precise detail, sits there, thumbing its nose at all those modern attempts to write it off as still another instance of the inflamed and disordered ancient imagination.

Beginning with Cuvier back in the eighteenth century, a succession of daring intellectual explorers have been braving the disapproval — sometimes the opprobrium and derision — of their academic colleagues, trying to account scientifically for these anomalies and to write the true scenario of the shattering events responsible for all those myths and legends.

The situation is like a gigantic jigsaw puzzle with most of the pieces originally missing. Early attempts to assemble the puzzle ended up with more holes than picture, and were relatively easy to ignore or dismiss. But as modern science develops, new pieces to the puzzle keep turning up. Successive attempts to put the whole picture together grow increasingly cogent.

The Flem-Aths are perhaps the most persuasive and daring of the contemporary "Atlantologists." Underpinned by the absolutely irrefutable fact of mass mammal extinctions around 10,000 B.C. and the precise, detailed, and no less irrefutable testimony of the Piri Re'is and other maps of the pre-catastrophe world, the picture becomes increasingly coherent. A spectrum of relevant disciplines — geology, paleoclimatology, cartography, astronomy, comparative religion — all contribute to the puzzle, and Hapgood's earth crust displacement theory seems to provide the *modus operandi* that accounts for the whole, huge, world-wide scenario in a single stroke.

Will the Flem-Aths' contemporary portrait finally take root and prevail? It is a big question. All of our human distant past hangs in the balance, along with the true story of the evolution of human civilization on earth.

Appendix

Rand Flem-Ath, "A Global Model for the Origins of Agriculture," *The Anthropological Journal of Canada*, vol. 19, no. 4 (1981), 2–7.
(Footnotes have been added to this previously published abstract.)

Abstract • A climatic model, based on archaeological evidence, is applied to the question of agricultural origins and the sequence of independent civilizations, on a global scale.

Why, one may ask, did agriculture become the preferred means of subsistence for mankind, following the termination of the Pleistocene? And, in the New World, why did it take so much longer for civilizations to develop? Early agricultural experiments here appear to be contemporary with those of the Old World, yet in certain respects they lagged far behind. It may be that we could gain a little insight with the aid of the poorly known climatic model of Hapgood (1970), in conjunction with the stress model of Harris (1977).

It has been argued by Cohen (1977), and rightly, that it is no longer adequate to explain just the "where" and the "when" of agricultural origins. More important by far is the "why" of the matter. What caused mankind, almost simultaneously in both Old and New Worlds, to shift from their highly successful and traditional hunting and gathering?

Global theories concerning this problem have fallen into three categories: 1) diffusion models; 2) population/ecological models; and 3) "traditional" climatic models. All have failed to account for major, significant archaeological evidence.

Agricultural origins are thought to fall around 10,000 to 11,000 years ago, well before the first civilizations, everywhere. This, with the evidence of Vavilov (1950) and Harlan (1971) for several centers of early agricultural experimentation, seriously undermines the concept of diffusion, in this regard. It becomes, in my view, untenable as a global model.[1]

It was E. Boserup (1965) who first put forward the idea of population density as a causal feature of technological change, thereby reversing the traditional Malthusian model. Following her, Cohen (1977) argued that population growth reached a worldwide saturation level, which in turn created a stress condition that forced the adoption of agriculture as a new strategy of food supply.

This thesis has three very serious drawbacks: 1) it flies in the face of anthropological data showing that hunter-gatherers normally maintain *equilibrium* with their environments; 2) given that the population density of the Old World was significantly greater than that of the New World, it fails to explain why the ecological thresholds were reached *at the same time*; and 3) it disregards the evidence of Vavilov, which shows a direct co-relation between high altitudes and the centers of greatest density of cultivated plants. In short, no light is shed on the "when" and "where" aspects of the problem.

Archaeological data are not well explained by diffusion and population/ecological global models. Let us, then, examine the "traditional" climatic theories. These have suffered from two problems: they are regional in scope and thus unable to account for the data on a broader perspective; and they are repetitive processes, leaving us to wonder why similar events in the past did not lead to agriculture.

Clearly, we need a theory to explain *why* agriculture began in the New and Old World at approximately the same time, yet led to such very different rates of cultural evolution. Such a theory must embrace the long-neglected correlation between altitude and centers, as well as [overcoming][2] the traditional limitations of [previous climatic models with their][3] repetitive and regional effects. And it must be *global*.

A climatic model, I feel, based on the geological theory of Charles H. Hapgood and the stress model of David Harris, can better answer

---

1 Diffusion from the Old World to the New World.
2 Corrected from the 1981 paper.
3 Corrected from the 1981 paper.

the questions raised above. It is indeed sad to say, in this light, that Hapgood's geological work has simply been ignored — even though the original volume (Hapgood 1958) was prefaced by the late Albert Einstein:

> A great many empirical data indicate that at each point on the earth's surface that has been carefully studied, many climatic changes have taken place, apparently quite suddenly. This, according to Mr. Hapgood, is explicable if the virtually rigid outer crust of the earth undergoes, from time to time, extensive displacement over the viscous, plastic, possibly fluid inner layers. Such displacements . . . will tend to alter the axis rotation of the earth's crust.

The earth's crustal displacement (ECD) referred to by Einstein is the shifting of various parts of the earth's crust, at different times, over the earth's axis.

Working on the assumption that the earth's magnetic poles are usually close to the poles of rotation, Hapgood collected geomagnetic rock samples, finding evidence that the most recent ECD must have occurred between 17,000 and 12,000 years ago. The North Pole would have moved from the Hudson Bay area of northern Canada to its current place in the Arctic Ocean. More recently, Langway and Hansen (1973) gathered climatic data pointing to a dramatic change in climate at 12,000 years ago. At that time, the Pleistocene extinctions, rising ocean levels, the close of the ice age, and the origins of agriculture all seem to coincide.

A displacement of the earth's crust, however dramatic, would have unequal impact in different areas. Some parts of the globe, which were tropical before the ECD of 12,000 B.P., remained so *after* the event. These I have labeled "Micro-Centers" (Figure 1).

Vavilov found a direct correlation between agricultural origins and lands more than 4,920 feet above sea level. This might be explained by crustal displacement, which would surely result in fantastic tidal waves. Any survivors would have a strong motive for staying in high mountains. Significantly, the Micro-Centers of Figure 1 lie above the suggested level.

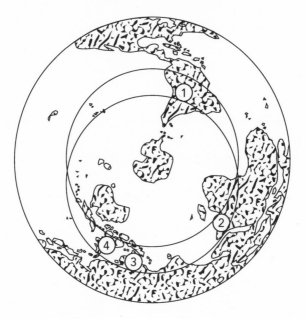

ECD-zones	before 12,000 B.P.	after 12,000 B.P.	Description of Lands
Micro-Centers	tropical	tropical	1. Central Andes 2. Ethiopian Highlands 3. Thailand Highlands 4. NE Borneo Highlands

Figure 1.

In three of the four Micro-Centers, agricultural developments have been dated to approximately 12,000 years ago. A number of studies in Peru, the highlands of Thailand, and near the Ethiopian highlands suggest to me that more excavations might be rewarding in the highlands of northeastern Borneo.

ECD creates a situation, says Hapgood, where mobility becomes limited, because large areas of the globe are temporarily uninhabitable. Harris (1977) argues that when hunter-gatherers begin to limit their mobility, they are inadvertently creating the conditions that lead to agriculture. According to this model, immobility creates population pressures. These intensify the difficulties of wild-food procurement, leading eventually to improved seasonal planning. Resource specialization, coupled with improved techniques and cultural selection of specific plants or animals, may develop into a

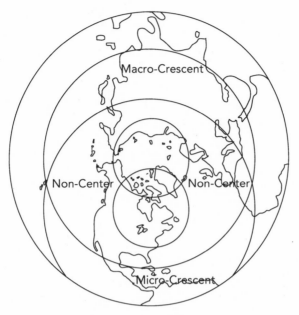

ECD-zones	before 12,000 B.P.	after 12,000 B.P.	Description of Lands
Macro-Crescent	tropical	temperate	Old World lands N of Tropic of Cancer and N of former T. of Can.
Micro-Crescent	temperate	tropical	North America S of T. of Cancer and N of former T. of Cancer.
Non-Center	temperate	temperate	North America N of T. of Cancer, Europe (not Crete & S. Greece), NW Africa, and Asia N of Tropic of Cancer

Figure 2.

genuine food-producing system. If, on the other hand, mobility is restored, a reversion to hunting-gathering can take place.

The model devised by Harris can also be applied to the areas in high altitudes that were temperate before and after the ECD of 12,000 B.P. (Figure 2).

The Non-Center area shown was just such a case. Mobility was quickly restored, as was the hunting-gathering subsistence pattern.

ECD-zones	before 12,000 B.P.	after 12,000 B.P.	Civilizations	Dates
Macro-Crescent	tropical	temperate	Sumeria Egypt Indus Minoan China	3500 B.C. 3200 B.C. 2600 B.C. 2100 B.C. 1800 B.C.
Micro-Crescent	temperate	tropical	Olmec	1200 B.C.
Micro-Center	tropical	tropical	Chavin	900 B.C.
Non-Center	temperate	temperate	none	none

Figure 3.

The area labeled Macro-Center, it is suggested, was most favorable for agricultural experiments at that time. It had been tropical, and was only newly temperate. Conditions for expansion into this zone from the Non-Center of the Old World were especially favorable. People who had gone almost all the way to food-producing, during a period of population pressures in the high mountains around the Black Sea, could move from a region that was temperate both before and after the ECD into a *newly* temperate zone. Such expansion would favor the use and development of agriculture.

Entirely different was the situation in the Micro-Crescent of the New World. Here, expansion to the south was into a zone that was formerly temperate, then became tropical. Human penetration was slow, because of the radically different climatic conditions encountered. In this very circumstance we find the reason for the time-lag in New World civilization (Figure 3).

The use of ECD to account for the sequence of early, independent civilizations can be seen in this figure. The first five, we note, appeared within the Macro-Crescent, while later societies fall into place according to the climatic conditions delineated. The first four civilizations were dependent upon plants and animals that were first domesticated near or in mountains, and in the vicinity of the Black Sea. China is seen as an offshoot of the highland Micro-Center of Thailand, which brought high-altitude plants from a tropical zone into a low-altitude temperate zone.

Why, then, did previous ECDs not lead to agriculture? I suggest that the explanation lies in two factors: 1) only two ECDs (12,000

B.P. and 55,000 B.P.) have occurred within the lifespan of *Homosapiens*;[4] and 2) because lower overall population levels in the past allowed for a reversion to hunting and gathering.

It is my conviction that the theory of earth crust displacement constitutes a scientific revolution in thinking as defined by Kuhn (1962). It is a theory that can be applied to various persistent problems in different scientific fields. In archaeology, it orders data on a *global* scale, and suggests new lines of investigation. Hapgood applied the theory to the problems of ice ages, mountain-building, extinctions, and the process of evolution. Recent developments in solar physics (Eddy 1978 and Gribbon 1980) are suggestive of a mechanism for the displacements.[5]

Herein, I have used the theory to explain the "why, where, and when" of agricultural origins, and the sequence of pristine civilizations. I hope to expand the model, eventually, to explain other problems in archaeology.

Received 15 May 1981

---

4 We now know that modern man has been with us a lot longer than was believed in 1981 (possibly in excess of 120,000 years).
5 These mechanisms have been abandoned in favor of the Croll/Milankovitch model, combined with the weight of the ice caps.

References

Boserup, E. 1965. *The Conditions of Agricultural Growth*. Chicago: Aldine.

Cohen, Mark N. 1977. *The Food Crisis in Prehistory: Overpopulation and the Origins of Agriculture*. New Haven, CT: Yale University Press.

Eddy, John A. 1978. Historical and Arboreal Evidence for a Changing Sun. In *The New Solar Physics*. Boulder, CO: Westview.

Gribbon, John. 1980. *The Strangest Star: A Scientific Account of the Life and Death of the Sun*. Glasgow: Fontana.

Hapgood, Charles H. 1958. *The Earth's Shifting Crust*. Philadelphia: Chilton.

————. 1970. *The Path of the Pole*. Philadelphia: Chilton.

Harlan, Jack R. 1971. Agricultural Origins: Centers and Noncenters. *Science* 174: 468–74.

Harris, Jack R. 1977. Alternative Pathways toward Agriculture. In *The Origins of Agriculture*, edited by C.A. Reed. The Hague: Mouton.

Kuhn, Thomas S. 1962. *The Structure of Scientific Revolutions*. Chicago: University of Chicago Press.

Langway, C.C. Jr., & B. Lyle Hansen. 1973. Drilling through the Ice Cap: Probing Climate for a Thousand Centuries. In *The Frozen Future: A Prophetic Report*, edited by Richard S. Lewis and P.M. Smith. New York: Quadrangle Books, 202.

Vavilov, N.I. 1950. The Origin, Variation, Immunity and Breeding of Cultivated Plants. Translated by K.S. Chester. *Chronica Botanica* 13 (1–6): 14–54.

Notes

Chapter One: Adapt, Migrate, or Die

1. Albert Einstein, Letter to Charles H. Hapgood, 8 May 1953. In Charles H. Hapgood, *The Path of the Pole*, 328. Philadelphia: Chilton Book Company, 1970.
2. Albert Einstein, in Hapgood, *Path of the Pole*, 341 n.5.
3. Albert Einstein, foreword to *The Earth's Shifting Crust; A Key to Some Basic Problems of Earth Science*, by Charles H. Hapgood (New York: Pantheon Books, 1958).
4. Thomas S. Kuhn, *The Structure of Scientific Revolutions*, 2nd Ed. (Chicago: University of Chicago Press, 1970).
5. John Horgan, "Profile: Reluctant Revolutionary: Thomas S. Kuhn unleashed 'paradigm' on the world," *Scientific American* 264 (May 1991): 40.
6. Kuhn, *Structure of Scientific Revolutions*, 5.
7. Charles H. Hapgood, *The Maps of the Ancient Sea Kings: Evidence of Advanced Civilization in the Ice Age.* (Philadelphia: Chilton Book Company, 1966).

Chapter Two: Embers of Humankind

1. Plato, *Laws*, vol. I, bk. III, trans. R.G. Bury (Cambridge, MA: Harvard University Press; London: William Heinemann Ltd., 1926), 167–73.
2. Jack R. Harlan, *Crops and Man* (Madison, WI: American Society of Agronomy and Crop Science Society of America, 1975), 35.

3. Alphonse de Candolle, *Origin of Cultivated Plants* (1886; reprint, New York: Hafner Pub. Co., 1959), 8.
4. Nikolai Ivanovich Vavilov, "The origin, variation, immunity and breeding of cultivated plants: Selected writings of N.I. Vavilov," trans. K. Starr Chester, *Chronica Botanica* 13, no. 1–6 (1951): 20.
5. *Ibid.*, 45.
6. Plato, in the *Laws*, claimed that agriculture began in the highlands after the Flood. He dates the Flood to 9600 B.C. (See Chapter Seven.)
7. Rand Flem-Ath, "A Global Model for the Origins of Agriculture," *Anthropological Journal of Canada* 19, no. 4 (1981): 2–7. (This article is reproduced in the Appendix.)
8. The tenth millennium B.C. is commonly regarded as the starting date for agriculture. See C.A. Reed, ed., *The Origins of Agriculture* (The Hague: Mouton, 1977).
9. Atlantis is focused upon in Chapters Seven and Eight.
10. Flem-Ath, "A Global Model."
11. *Ibid.*

Chapter Three: The Wayward Sun

1. Major J.W. Powell, "Mythologic Philosophy," *Popular Science Monthly* 15 (1880): 795–808.
2. Franz Boas, *Kutenai Tales*, Smithsonian Institution; Bureau of American Ethnology, Bulletin 59 (Government Printing Office, Washington, D.C.: 1918), 281.
3. *Ibid.*, 287.
4. Harry Robert Turney-High, *Ethnology of the Kutenai* (Mildwood, NY: Draus Reprint Co., 1974), 96.
5. Paul E. Baker, *The Forgotten Kuetenai* (Boise, ID: Mountain States Press, 1955), 7.
6. British Columbia, *Kootney*, vol. 8 of *Our Native People*, Department of Education, Division of Curriculum, series 1952–62 (Victoria, B.C., 1952), 12.
7. Turney-High, *Ethnology of the Kutenai*, 11–12.

8. Boas, *Kutenai Tales*, 281.
9. Boas, *Kutenai Tales*, 231.
10. Hubert Howe Bancroft, *The Native Races*, vol. III (San Francisco: The History Co., 1886), 153–54.
11. Robert H. Lowie, *Anthropological Papers of the American Museum of Natural History*, vol. XX, part III (New York: American Museum Press, 1924), 293.
12. Penelope Farmer, *Beginnings: Creation Myths of the World* (London: Chatto & Windus, 1978), 127.
13. *Dictionary of Indian Tribes of the Americas*, vol. 3 (Newport Beach, CA: American Indian Publishers, Inc.) 455–60.
14. Philip Freund, *Myths of Creation* (New York: Washington Square Press Inc., 1965), 11.
15. Fredrick Dockstader, "Pima," in *Dictionary of Indian Tribes of the Americas*, vol. 22 (Newport Beach, CA: American Indian Publishers, Inc.).
16. Raymond Van Over, ed., *Sun Songs: Creation Myths from Around the World* (New York: A Mentor Book of the New American Library, 1980), 30–31.
17. *Ibid.*, 28.
18. *The Mythology of All Races*, vol. X (New York: Cooper Square Publishers, Inc., 1964), 222.
19. Ella E. Clark, *Indian Legends of the Pacific Northwest* (Berkeley and Los Angeles: University of California Press, 1953), 42–43.
20. *Ibid.*, 14–15.
21. *Ibid.*, 31–32.
22. Roland Dixon, "Achomawial Atsugewi Tales," *Journal of American Folk-Lore* 21 (1908): 169.
23. Roland Dixon, "Ahasta Myths," *Journal of American Folk-Lore* 23 (1910): 36.
24. James Mooney, *Myths of the Cherokee*, American Bureau of Ethnology Annual Report Part I (Washington, D.C.: Government Printing Office, 1900), 252–54.
25. William Tyler Olcott, *Sun Lore of All Ages* (New York: The Knickerbocker Press; London: G.P. Putnam's Sons, 1914), 60.
26. Bancroft, *The Native Races*, vol. III, 154.
27. Freund, *Myths of Creation*, 10.

28. *New Larouse Encyclopedia of Mythology* (London and New York: Prometheus press, 1968), 445.

29. Augustin de Zarate, *The Discovery and Conquest of Peru* (1555; reprint, Middlesex, England: Penguin Books, 1968), 49.

30. Hartley Burr Alexander, *Latin America*, vol. XI of *The Mythology of All Races* (New York: Cooper Square, 1964), 202.

31. Pedro de Cieza de Leon, *The Incas of Pedro de Cieza de Leon*, trans. Harriet de Onis (Norman, OK: University of Oklahoma Press, 1959), 27.

32. A.F. Banelier, *The Islands of Titicaca and Koati*, as reprinted in Thor Heyerdahl, *American Indians in the Pacific; The Theory Behind the Kon-Tiki Expedition* (London: George Allen and Unwin, 1952), 257.

33. Hiram Bingham, "The Story of Machu Picchu," *National Geographic*, February 1915, 183.

34. *Ibid.*, 181.

35. *Ibid.*, 185.

36. Ibid., 183.

37. Hiram Bingham, *Lost City of the Incas* (New York: Duell, Sloan and Pearce, 1948), 35.

38. "The Anasazi," *National Geographic*, November 1982, 580–81. See also; Anna Sofaer, *The Sun Dagger*, a film produced by the Solstice Project, Washington, D.C., 1982, Bullfrog Films, directed by Albert Ihde and written by Anna Sofaer (narrated by Robert Redford).

39. John A. MacCulloch and Jan Machal, *Celtic, Slavic*, vol. III of *The Mythology of All Races* (New York: Cooper Square Publishers, Inc., 1964), 12.

40. Raymond Van Over, ed., *Sun Songs; Creation Myths from Around the World* (New York: A Mentor Book of the New American Library, 1980), 165.

41. Uno Homberg, *Finno-Ugric, Siberian*, vol. IV of *The Mythology of All Races* (New York: Cooper Square Publishers, Inc., 1964), 312.

42. W. Max Muller, *Egypt, Far East*, vol. XII of *The Mythology of All Races* (New York: Cooper Square Publishers, Inc., 1964), 82.

43. *Ibid.*, 39.

44. J.M. Plumley, "The Cosmology of Ancient Egypt," in *Ancient Cosmologies*, ed. Carmen Blacker and Michael Loewe (London: George Allen & Unwin, 1975), 25–26.

45. G.S. Kirk and J.E. Raven, *The Presocratic Philosophers* (Cambridge: Cambridge University Press, 1957), 13.

Chapter Four: Why the Sky Fell

1. Georges Cuvier, in Robert Silverberg, *Mammoths, Mastodons and Man* (New York: McGraw-Hill Book Co., 1970), 101.

2. Georges Cuvier, "Revolutions and Catastrophes in the History of the Earth," in *A Source Book in Geology*, ed. K. Mather (New York and London: Hafner Pub. Co., 1964) facsimile of the 1939 edition by Harvard University Press, 11.

3. Edward Lurie, *Louis Agassiz: A Life in Science* (Chicago: University of Chicago Press, 1960), 63–64.

4. Gordon L. Davies, *The Earth in Decay: A History of British Geomorphology* 1578–1878 (London: Macdonald Technical & Scientific, 1969), 6.

5. James Hutton, *Theory of the Earth with Proofs and Illustrations*, vol. I (Edinburgh: William Creech; London: Cadell, Junior and Davies, 1795), 275.

6. *Ibid.*, 273.

7. *Ibid.*, vol. II, 547

8. Charles Lyell, *Principles of Geology: Being an Attempt to Explain the Former Changes of the Earth's Surface, by Reference to Causes Now in Operation*, vol. III (London: John Murray, 1830–32), 2–3.

9. Stephen Jay Gould, "Is Uniformitarianism Necessary?," *American Journal of Science* 263, no. 3 (March 1965): 223–28.

10. Louis Agassiz, as quoted in Ruth Moore, *The Earth We Live On: The Story of Geological Discovery*, 2nd rev. ed. (New York: Knopf, 1971), 140.

11. Louis Agassiz, in Edward Lurie, *Louis Agassiz*, 98.

12. Louis Agassiz, *Geological Sketches*, vol. I (Boston, Ticknor & Fields, 1866), 210.

13. James Croll, in John Imbrie and Katherine Palmer Imbrie, *Ice*

Ages: Solving the Mystery (Short Hills, NJ: Enslow Publishers, 1979), 80.

14. J.D. Hays, J. Imbrie, and N.J. Schackleton, "Variations in the earth's orbit: pacemaker of the ice ages," Science 194 (1976): 1121–32.

15. Albert Einstein, foreword to The Earth's Shifting Crust, as reproduced in Charles H. Hapgood, The Path of the Pole (Philadelphia: Chilton Book Company, 1970), xiv.

16. Alfred Russel Wallace, The World of Life: A Manifestation of Creative Power, Directive Mind, and Ultimate Purpose (New York: Moffat, Yard, 1911), 264.

17. Charles Lyell, as quoted in James J. Hester, "The Agency of Man in Animal Extinctions," in P.S. Martin and H.E. Wright, Jr., eds., Pleistocene Extinctions: The Search for a Cause (New Haven, CT: Yale University Press, 1967), 189.

18. Paul S. Martin, "Prehistoric Overkill: The Global Model," in Paul S. Martin and Richard G. Klein, Quaternary Extinctions: A Prehistoric Revolution (Tucson, AZ: The University of Arizona Press, 1984), 396.

19. N.K. Vereschagin and G.F. Baryshnikov, "Quaternary Mammal Extinctions in Northern Eurasia," in Paul S. Martin and Richard G. Klein, Quaternary Extinctions: A Prehistoric Revolution (Tucson, AZ: The University of Arizona Press, 1984), 483–516.

20. Anthony Stuart, "Who (or what) killed the giant armadillo?," New Scientist III, no. 1517 (17 July, 1986): 29–32.

21. Paul S. Martin, "Prehistoric Overkill," 396.

22. Paul S. Martin and Richard G. Klein, eds., Quaternary Extinctions: A Prehistoric Revolution (Tucson; AZ: The University of Arizona Press, 1984).

23. Ibid.

Chapter Five: The Lost Island Paradise

1. Hartley Burr Alexander, North America, vol. X of The Mythology of All Races (New York: Cooper Square Publishers, Inc., 1964), 249–50.

2. Brian M. Fagan, *The Great Journey: The Peopling of Ancient America* (New York: Thames and Hudson, 1987), 141.
3. Marius Barbeau, *Haida Myths: Illustrated in Argillite Carvings*, Bulletin No. 127, Anthropological Series No. 32 (Ottawa: National Museum of Canada, 1953), 187.
4. Joseph Greenberg, Christy Turner, and Stephen Zegura, "The Settlement of the Americas: A Comparison of the Linguistic, Dental, and Genetic Evidence," *Current Anthropology* 27, no. 5 (1986): 479.
5. Merritt Ruhlen, "Voices from the Past," *Natural History* (March 1987): 10.
6. Andrew M.T. Moore, "A Pre-Neolithic Farmer's Village on the Euphrates," *Scientific American* 241 (August 1979): 62–70.
7. *New Larouse Encyclopedia of Mythology* introduction by Robert Graves (London: Prometheus Press, 1968), 55.
8. *Ibid.*, p. 62.
9. Louis Herbert Gray, *The Mythology of All Races*, vol. VI (New York: Cooper Square Pub. Inc., 1964), 208.
10. *New Larouse Encyclopedia of Mythology* (London: Prometheus Press, 1968), 62.
11. Geoffrey Bibby, *Looking for Dilmun* (New York: Knopf, 1969), Chapter Two.
12. Arthur Posnansky, *Tihuanacu, the Cradle of American Man*, vol. I, trans. James F. Shearer (New York: J.J. Augustin, 1945), 11.
13. *Ibid.*, 89–90.
14. John Anthony West, *Serpent in the Sky: The High Wisdom of Ancient Egypt* (Wheaton, IL: First Quest Edition, 1993).
15. Paul William Roberts, "Riddle of the Sphinx," *Saturday Night* (March 1993): 27.
16. Robert Bauval and Adrian Gilbert, *The Orion Mystery: Are the Pyramids a Map of Heaven?* (London: Atrium Press, 1994).
17. Weston La Berre, "The Aymara Indians of the Lake Titicaca Plateau, Bolivia," *American Anthropologist* 50 (1948): 9.
18. Cieza de Leon, as quoted in Thor Heyerdahl, *American Indians in the Pacific: The Theory Behind the Kon-Tiki Expedition* (London: George Allen and Unwin, 1952), 231.
19. Paul Mylrea, "Computer helps preserve ancient Aymara

language," as reprinted in *The Nanaimo Free Press*, 21 November 1991, p. 8.

20. John Barnes, "Ancient purity and polyglot programs," *Sunday Times* (London), 4 November 1984, Computing section, p. 13.
21. Posnansky, *Tihuanacu*, 2.
22. Based on C.A. Burland, *Montezuma: Lord of Aztecs* (New York: G.P. Putnam's & Sons, 1973), Chapters Six and Ten; and Maurice Collins, *Cortes and Montezuma* (London: Faber & Faber, 1954), Chapter Five.
23. Burland, *Montezuma*, 183.
24. *Ibid.*, 165.
25. Posnansky, *Tihuanacu*, 182.
26. Burland, *Montezuma*, 169–70.
27. Collins, *Cortes and Montezuma*, 56–60.
28. Bernal Diaz del Castillo, *The Discovery and Conquest of Mexico 1517–1521*, trans. Irving A. Leonard (New York: Farrar, Straus and Company, 1956), 32.
29. Hubert Howe Bancroft, *The Native Races*, vol. III (San Francisco: The History Co., 1886; reprint, Arno & McGraw-Hill Book Co., New York, n.d.), 469.
30. Burr Cartwright Brundage, *The Fifth Sun: Aztec Gods, Aztec World* (Austin, TX: University of Texas Press, 1979), 6.
31. John L. Sorenson, "The Significance of an Apparent Relationship between the Ancient Near East and Mesoamerica," in Carroll L. Riley et al., eds., *Man Across the Sea: Problems of Pre-Columbia Contacts* (Austin, TX: University of Texas Press, 1971), 239.
32. Ignatius Donnelly, *Atlantis: the Antediluvian World* (New York: Harper, 1882), 326.
33. Robin Palmer, *Dictionary of Mythical Places* (1920; reprint, New York: Henry Z. Walck, Inc., 1975).
34. Alexander, 113–14.
35. W.H. Prescott, *History of the Conquest of Mexico and History of the Conquest of Peru* (1843; reprint, New York: Modern Library, 1936), 693.
36. Lee Eldridge Huddlesten, *Origins of the American Indians:*

European Concepts 1492–1729 (Austin, TX: University of Texas Press, 1967), 56.

37. William L. Shirer, *Gandhi: A Memoir* (New York: Washington Square Press, 1979), 85.

38. Bal Gangadhar Tilak, *The Arctic Home in the Vedas: Being also a new key to the interpretation of many Vedic texts and legends* (Poona City, India: Kesari, 1903), 419.

39. *Ibid.*, 72.

40. William Fairfield Warren, *Paradise Found: The Cradle of the Human Race at the North Pole; A Study of the Prehistoric World* (Boston: Houghton, Mifflin & Co., 1885) 193–96.

41. *Ibid.*, 141.

42. *Ibid.*, 140–41.

43. *Ibid.*, 225.

Chapter Six: A Land Forgotten

1. Associated Press, "Bear-bones find challenges idea of when Ice Age began in Norway," 23 August 1993.

2. Donald G. Sutherland and Michael J.C. Walker, "A Late Devensian ice-free area and possible interglacial site on the Isle of Lewis, Scotland," *Nature* 309 (1984): 701–3.

3. R. Dale Guthrie, "Mammals of the Mammoth Steppe as Paleo-environmental Indicators," in David M. Hopkins et al., *The Paleoecology of Beringia* (New York: Academic Press, 1982), 309.

4. *Ibid.*, 41.

5. *Ibid.*, 65.

6. Boris A. Yurtsev, "Relics of the Xerophyte Vegetation of Beringia in Northeastern Asia," in Hopkins et al., *Paleoecology*, 157.

7. J.V. Matthew Jr., *American Quaternary Association Abstracts*, 1976, 73–77.

8. A.P. Okladnikov, *Yakutia Before its Incorporation into the Russian State*, ed. H.N. Michael (Montreal: McGill-Queen's University Press, 1970).

9. N.K. Vereschagin and G.F. Baryshnikov, "Quaternary Mammal Extinctions in Northern Eurasia," in Paul S. Martin and Richard G. Klein, *Quaternary Extinctions: A Prehistoric Revolution* (Tucson, AZ: The University of Arizona Press, 1984), 483–516.

10. Charles H. Hapgood, *The Path of the Pole* (Philadelphia: Chilton Book Company, 1970), 256.

11. Ray Nelson, "Evidence of the Earliest Americans," *Popular Science* (March 1994): 28.

12. The Pacific route to America was open, according to the theory proposed here, from 80,000 to 20,000 years ago. From 20,000 to 11,600 years ago, the conditions would have deteriorated due to the expansion of the ice sheet centred on Hudson Bay. Passage after 11,600 years ago was once again possible.

Chapter Seven: From Atlantis

1. Plato, *The Timaeus of Plato*, trans. R.D. Archer-Hind (London: Macmillan & Co., 1888), 65.

2. Plutarch, *The Lives of the Noble Grecians and Romans* (retitled (*The Rise and Fall of Athens*), trans. Ian Scott-Kilvert (Middlesex, England: Penguin Books, 1960), 54–55.

3. *Ibid.*, 68.

4. *Ibid.*, 69.

5. Plato, *Timaeus, Critias, Cletophon, Menexenus, Epistles*, trans. R.D. Bury (1929; reprint, Cambridge, MA: Harvard University Press; London: William Heinemann Ltd., 1975), 37, 39.

6. These clues have been derived from Plato's dialogues *Timaeus and Critias*.

7. Pindar, in E.H. Warmington, *Greek Geography*, (London and Toronto: J.M. Dent & Sons Ltd., 1934), 77.

8. Aristotle, *On the Universe*, in E.H. Warmington, *Greek Geography* (London and Toronto: J.M. Dent & Sons, 1934), 208.

9. William A. Anikouchine and Richard W. Sternberg, *The World Ocean: An Introduction to Oceanography* (Englewood Cliffs, NJ: Prentice-Hall, 1973), 2.

10. Plato, *Timaeus* (three translations)
    The Timaeus of Plato, edited with an introduction and notes by R.D. Archer-Hind (London: Macmillan & Co., 1888), 69–70.
    Timaeus, Critias, Cletophon, Menexenus, Epistles, trans. R.D. Bury (1929; reprint, Cambridge, MA: Harvard University Press; and London: William Heinemann Ltd., 1973), 31–33.
    Timaeus and Critias, trans. Desmond Lee (Middlesex, England: Penguin Books, 1965), 34–35.
11. Plato, *Timaeus of Plato*, 70; *Timaeus, Critias, Cletophon*, 33; *Timaeus and Critias*, 35.
12. Plato, *Timaeus and Critias*, n.8, 141.
13. Joseph Whitaker, *Almanack for the Year of our Lord* 1992 (London: J. Whitaker and Sons, Ltd., 1992), 1176.
14. *Encyclopedia Americana: International Edition*, vol. 7 (Danbury, CT: Grolier Incorporated, 1986), 688.
15. Plato, *The Timaeus of Plato*, ed. R.D. Archer-Hind, n.8, 69–70.
16. Plato, *Timaeus of Plato*, 79; *Timaeus, Critias, Cletophon*, 41; *Timaeus and Critias*, 37.
17. The following description of the city and location of the city of Atlantis are based upon Plato's dialogue *Critias*.
18. Plato, *Timaeus, Critias, Cletophon*, 301.
19. *Ibid.*, 303.
20. *Ibid.*, 283.

Chapter Eight: Atlantean Maps

1. Muhammad ibn Ishaq ibn al-Nadim, *The Fihrist of al-Nadim; a tenth century survey of Muslim culture*, vol. II, ed. and trans. Baynard Dodge (New York: Columbia University Press, 1970), 583.
2. *Ibid.*, 584.
3. Charles H. Hapgood, *Maps of the Ancient Sea Kings: Evidence of Advanced Civilization in the Ice Age* (Philadelphia: Chilton Book Company, 1966), 41–42, 101.
4. A.A. Vasiliev, *History of the Byzantine Empire 324–1453* (Madison, WI: University of Wisconsin Press, 1952), 452.

5. Ibid., 453.
6. Ibid., 459.
7. Ibid., 461.
8. Sir Henry Yule, *The Book of Ser Marco Polo*, 2 vols. (1870; reprint, London; John Murray, 1921), 5.
9. George Kish, ed., *A Source Book in Geography* (Cambridge, MA: Harvard University Press, 1978), 128.
10. Elaine Sanceau, *Henry the Navigator* (New York: Archon Books, 1969) 117.
11. Ian Cameron, *Lodestone and Evening Star: The Epic Voyages of Discovery* 1493 B.C.–1896 A.D. (New York: E.P. Dutton & Co., Inc., 1966), 107.
12. Sanceau, *Henry the Navigator*, 111.
13. Hapgood, *Maps of the Ancient Sea Kings*, Chapters One to Three.
14. Ibid., Chapter Four.
15. Samuel Eliot Morison, *Admiral of the Ocean Sea* (Boston: Little, Brown and Co., 1942), 39.
16. Edward Gaylord Bourne, *Spain in America* (New York: Harper & Brothers, 1904; reprint, New York: Barnes & Noble, Inc., 1962), 119.
17. Lt. Colonel Harold Z. Ohlmeyer (United States Air Force), letter to Charles H. Hapgood, 6 July 1960, in Hapgood, *Maps of the Ancient Sea Kings*, 243.
18. Ibid., Preface.
19. Conor (S.J.) Reilly, "Father Athanasius Kircher, S.J., Master of an Hundred Arts," *Studies: An Irish Quarterly Review* 44 (1955): 459.
20. Ibid., 460.
21. Ibid., 458.
22. Ibid., 460–61.

Chapter Nine: Mythology Unmasked

1. Diogenes Laertius, *Lives of Eminent Philosophers*, vol. I, trans. R.D. Hicks (London: Heinemann, 1925), 29.
2. Ibid., 37.

3. Giambattista Vico, *The New Science of Giambattista Vico*, trans. Thomas Goddard Bergin and Max Harold Fisch (Ithaca, NY: Cornell University Press, 1948), 68.
4. *Ibid.*, 57.
5. *Ibid.*, 60.
6. Edward B. Tylor, *Primitive Culture: Researches into the Development of Mythology, Philosophy, Religion, Art and Custom*, 2 vols. (London: John Murray, 1871), 255–56.
7. Sigmund Freud, *Psychopathology of Everyday Life*, vol. VI of *The Standard Edition of the Complete Psychological Works of Sigmund Freud* (London: Hogarth Press, 1960), 47–48.
8. Carl G. Jung and C. Kerenyi, *Introduction to a Science of Mythology* (London: Routledge & Kegan Paul Ltd., 1970), 102–3.
9. Claude Lévi-Strauss, *Structural Anthropology*, trans. Claire Jacobson and Brooke Grundfest Schoepf (New York: Basic Books: Middlesex, England: Allan Lane, 1963), 229.
10. Joseph Campbell, *The Hero With a Thousand Faces*, 2nd ed., (Princeton, NJ: Princeton University Press, 1968), 4.
11. Thomas S. Kuhn, *The Essential Tension* (Chicago: University of Chicago Press, 1977), Chapter One.
12. Laertius, *Lives of Eminent Philosophers*, vol. II, 343.
13. Ovid, *Metamorphoses*, trans. Mary M. Innes (Middlesex, England: Penguin Books, 1955), 341.
14. Strabo, *The Geography of Strabo*, trans. H.C. Hamilton (London: G. Bell and Sons Ltd., 1912), 154.
15. Proclus, *The Commentaries of Proclus on the Timaeus of Plato, in Five Books: Containing a Treasure of Pythagoric and Platonic Physiology*, vol. I, bk. I, trans. Thomas Taylor (London: author, 1820), 64.
16. Ignatius Donnelly, *Atlantis: The Antediluvian World* (New York: Harper & Brothers, 1882), 1.
17. *Ibid.*, 2.
18. John Anthony West, *Mystery of the Sphinx*, a television documentary hosted by Charlton Heston (A Magic Eye/North Tower Films Production, U.S.A., 1993).
19. Time-Life Books, *Mystic Places* (Alexandria, VA: Time-Life Books, 1987), 23.
20. Charles Lyell, *Principles of Geology: Being an Attempt to Explain the*

Former Changes of the Earth's Surface, by Reference to Causes Now in Operation, vol. III (London: John Murray, 1830–32), 2–3.

21. J.V. Luce, *The End of Atlantis: New Light on an Old Legend* (London: Thames and Hudson, 1969).

22. Harald A. Reiche, "The Language of Archaic Astronomy: A Clue to the Atlantis Myth?," in *Astronomy of the Ancients*, ed. Kenneth Brecher and Michael Feirtag (Cambridge, MA: The MIT Press, 1979), 176.

23. West, *Mystery of the Sphinx*.

24. Graham Hancock, *The Sign and the Seal: The Quest for the Lost Ark of the Covenant*, a Touchstone Book (New York: Simon & Schuster, Inc., 1992), photograph no. 4. (This obelisk was probably built using technology from Atlantis.)

25. John Anthony West, "New eyes on the Nile," in *Condé Nast Traveler* (January 1994): 125.

26. *Ibid.*, 122.

27. See Aymara language in Chapter Five.

28. See Chapter Two.

ndex